ABOUT THE AUTHOR

Shen Ming Lee is an author, entrepreneur, and ecosystem builder passionate about agri-food tech and social impact. Through her work, Shen supports agri-food innovation, tackles pressing food issues, and advocates for tech innovations in a better food future. Ultimately, she aims to help build thriving ecosystems that can support a more sustainable, connected, and innovative food system.

As a thought leader, Shen regularly speaks about agri-food innovation and entrepreneurship and has spoken at conferences & corporate events like TEDx, CGIAR's Global Food Security Symposium, Future Food Asia, YPO, South China Morning Post's Asia Sustainability Conference, and more.

A lover of all things gastronomy, Shen grew up in Malaysia and went to the Cornell University School of Hotel Administration to pursue her undergraduate studies. In her free time, Shen loves to cook, bake, box, and cycle. You can learn more about Shen's work at www.shenminglee.com.

PRAISE FOR SHEN MING LEE'S
HUNGRY FOR DISRUPTION

"Shen Ming Lee skillfully shows that a key to food sustainability in the 21st century is advancing food technology so we can produce more with less. If you love delicious food and want there to be enough for everyone, Lee asks you to cheer on the scientists who are working hard to keep us fed while leaving a lighter footprint on our planet."

> — Paul Shapiro, CEO of The Better Meat Co. and author of the Washington Post bestseller *Clean Meat: How Growing Meat Without Animals Will Revolutionize Dinner and the World*

"Brilliantly elucidates a problem as complex as our broken food system. Shen's personal experience as a Malaysian Chinese brings unique perspective and breadth to this insightful account on how technology can create that urgently needed paradigm shift for all, at whatever stage of development, towards 2050."

> —Elaine Siu, Managing Director of The Good Food Institute Asia Pacific

"Our next big challenge is on our plate. Shen delivers a vibrant testimony to the power of technology to address it. If eating is as much of a cultural act as an agricultural one, her book has the power to cross borders and inspire a new breed of entrepreneurs from around the world."

> —Isabelle Decitre, Founder & CEO of ID Capital & Future Food Asia

"By delivering an expansive exploration of the world of food and agriculture technologies, Shen gives us hope that the future of feeding the world could be a sustainable, efficient, and delicious one... a bold and compelling vision of what the global food and agricultural systems will look like towards 2050."

> —Dr. Prabhu Pingali, Director of the Tata-Cornell Institute for Agriculture & Nutrition and Professor of Applied Economics at Cornell University

"The global food supply chain is broken and in need of large-scale disruption. Shen Ming Lee details the challenges of the current system while providing hope for its improvement through technology and innovation."

"An eye-opening account of some of the most transformative quiet revolutions that will feed humanity."

"Our food system is rife with problems, but in these lie enormous opportunities. Shen Ming Lee clearly shows us how technology and innovation are transforming the future of food, and solving our planet's most pressing challenges along the way."

"Shen Ming Lee pulled together a remarkable project that analyzes disruptive technologies that address the world's food challenges. Anyone that is in the Food & Ag playground should read this macro-data book".

"Shen has taken some complex issues in the world of agriculture and made them easy for all to understand."

HUNGRY FOR DISRUPTION

HOW TECH INNOVATIONS WILL
NOURISH 10 BILLION BY 2050

SHEN MING LEE

NEW DEGREE PRESS

HUNGRY FOR DISRUPTION

How Tech Innovations Will Nourish 10 Billion By 2050

ISBN   978-1-64137-208-4 *Paperback*

        978-1-64137-209-1 *Ebook*

For the farmers, entrepreneurs, investors, scientists, activists, chefs, and innovators who are building a more sustainable, food secure, equitable, and delicious tomorrow.

CONTENTS

FOREWORD

———

BY PRABHU PINGALI

We are facing a "perfect storm" of global threats and challenges that need agri-food R&D and policy solutions. Some of the dominant challenges faced by the global community are unabated population growth, rising urbanization, the growing epidemic of non-communicable diseases, climate change risks, and environmental degradation. These global threats are being felt contemporaneously and their combined effects are greater than the sum of their individual effects. There are also emerging opportunities for future food and agricultural systems that can positively contribute to rural prosperity; improvements in nutrition and environmental sustainability, including enhanced management of climate threats.

While we live in a world of never-ending challenges, we also live in one where the pace of scientific research and technological advances are unprecedented. Without scientific and technological advances, the world's potential to face the above challenges is weak. Innovations in biotechnology and gene-editing, the internet of things (IoT), precision agriculture, alternative protein research, and technologies that improve food safety and reduce food waste, are poised to play a massive role in enhancing the agri-food systems of our future. Substantive policy action, extensive research, and technological investments will ensure that a rising global population approaching 10 billion can be fed sustainably and equitably.

The future of the agri-food sector will be shaped by a range of innovations and disruptive technologies that the world has only begun to grasp. Disruptive technological breakthroughs are most likely in enhancing agricultural resource use efficiency, such as energy and water, and in post-harvest operations for enhancing quality and safety. The use of agricultural drones and the spread of vertical farming are two such examples of disruptive innovations that can have a transformative impact on food systems. If applied in the right contexts, these innovations have the potential to improve global nutrition, promote environmental sustainability, and contribute to pressing areas of development like poverty and inequality. These technological innovations also have significant potential to leapfrog developing countries towards the adoption of modern agricultural systems.

In a future wrought with uncertainty in feeding the world well and meeting our climate goals, Shen's book, *Hungry for Disruption: How Tech Innovations Will Nourish 10 Billion by 2050*, provides a futuristic look into how scientific and technological advances will affect our future food systems. As the world's population reaches 10 billion people by 2050, the challenges for humankind remain unsettling. With urgent pressures put on our food systems, we must harness the power of science and technology to transform global agriculture. This book unlocks that power. By delivering an expansive exploration of the world of food and agriculture technologies, Shen gives us hope that the future of feeding the world could be a sustainable, efficient, and delicious one.

I am extremely impressed that Shen, an undergraduate student at Cornell University, has provided us with such a bold and compelling vision of what the global food and agricultural systems will look like towards 2050. If her vision is correct, we are on our way to a better global future, one in which we should see significant gains in nutrition, health, and environmental sustainability. As someone just starting off in her career, Shen will have a front row seat in seeing global change happening and her vision come to reality.

PRABHU PINGALI
Professor of Applied Economics & Director of the
Tata-Cornell Institute for Agriculture & Nutrition
Cornell University, Ithaca, New York

THE FUTURE OF FOOD MISSION

———

I grew up in Kuala Lumpur, Malaysia, in a privileged, loving home. Growing up, food was never an issue and in fact, it was abundant. On celebratory occasions and family meals, the table was always filled with all sorts of delicacies. I remember relishing Saturday lunches at my grandma's house with her famous Roast Pork with applesauce. My mum's homemade Bolognese will always bring back good memories. Like many, my earliest food memories revolve around everything home cooked. Home cooked food serves as a reminder of what home means to me and most importantly, what my mum and grandma's love and nurture feels like.

Growing up in such a foodie home, I developed an intense love for cooking and baking at a very young age.

When I was 8, I was already helping chop onions and stir-fry vegetables in the kitchen. When I was 10, I started selling my homemade cupcakes at a local sundry store. When I was 17, I started a farm-to-table, supper club restaurant in Singapore to pursue my passion for cooking, educate people about real food, and raise awareness about the Malaysian Myanmar Refugee crisis.

My passion for food really began with a love for cooking & hospitality. When I came to the U.S. to pursue this passion at the Cornell School of Hotel Administration, my dream was to start a health food chain. This stemmed from seeing people around me happily eat McDonald's 3-5 times a week and me feeling incredibly grateful that my mother taught me the importance of my 5 servings of fruit and vegetables a day. My goal was simply to change people's perceptions of food. To show them that real food was better than fake food.

Over the last few years, my perspective of food and how we play a role in our food system started to change. In my first year of university, I took a class on food injustice and it deeply affected me. My final paper explored the effects of U.S. farm subsidies on the fight for food justice. I remember learning how the rise of large agribusinesses resulted in increasing corporate control of our food system. I remember discovering that corn subsidies perpetuated gross inequality in our food system. I remember being shocked to learn that while the U.S. Department of Agriculture (USDA) spent more than US$13 billion on farm subsidies in 2017,[1] more than 90% of those subsidies went to 5 major crops – wheat, cotton, corn, soybeans, and rice.[2] Meanwhile, no subsidies were given to producers of fruit, vegetables, beef, or poultry. It is an understatement to say that I felt a deep sense of injustice and discomposure.

Later on, I worked on an agriculture technology project at Cornell Venture Capital, which really opened my eyes to how technology could provide tremendous opportunities and solutions for our most dire food production problems. Inevitable issues like increasing urbanization, massive food supply chain inefficiency, climate change, and falling farmer incomes demanded better food production solutions. Suddenly, food became more than just cooking and hospitality for me. Clearly, food was a lot more.

The excitement I felt discovering emerging food and agriculture technologies coupled with my knowledge of pressing global food issues left me devastated and confused, but also remarkably optimistic. I started becoming deeply curious about how technological innovations like cell-cultured meat provided solutions to our most pressing food production problems. I remember reading up on plant-based meat companies like Beyond Meat and indoor farming companies like BrightFarms and thinking: "Wow. Everything about the food system is going to change. It will need to change. I want to find out how." So, with that curiosity, I set out on a mission to explore how technology and innovative ways of thinking could help us nourish almost 10 billion people on this planet by 2050.

This mission has brought me to the wildest of discoveries and the craziest of adventures. I've talked to dozens of food and agriculture experts, entrepreneurs at the cusp of cutting-edge food and agriculture technologies, and investors funding the next agri-food tech revolution. I've walked through rows of hydroponic, vertically grown kale, and feasted on insects, plant-based meat, and micro-algae based products at food tech conferences.

From skipping a midterm exam in order to attend the Future of Food conference to the shocking realization that we could either genetically engineer cows or feed them seaweed to belch and fart less (and therefore produce less methane—a key greenhouse gas), I hope you're as excited as I am for you to join me in this exploration of how technological innovation can help us create a better, more sustainable, and inclusive food system.

NOURISHING THE WORLD IN 2050

———

In a vast potato field in Reusel, Netherlands, Dutch farmer Jacob Van den Borne sits in the cabin of an immense tractor equipped with a machine panel reminiscent of *Star Trek's* starship *Enterprise*.[1]

From his agricultural throne 10 feet above the ground, he's monitoring two drones—a driverless tractor roaming the fields and an unmanned quad copter flying in the air—that provide detailed information on soil quality, water content, nutrient levels, and growth. Armed with this information, Van den Borne can monitor the progress of every plant down to the individual potato.

While the global average yield of potatoes is nine tons per acre, Van den Borne's farm consistently produces more than

20 tons per acre.[2] It's no surprise that he's dubbed the "Elon Musk of Potatoes" and the "Pope of Precision Agriculture."

A third-generation farmer, Van den Borne is the epitome of a modern, tech-savvy farmer. His technology stack combines data analytics from soil sensing systems, satellite imaging, and yield monitoring systems in order to optimize his crop's growth. For instance, his biomass sensors help him to better fulfill the needs of each individual plant, rather than treating the whole field the same. The result is that he's reduced both fertilizer and herbicide use by 20%, all whilst achieving a 1% annual average yield increase since taking over the farm in 2006.[3]

Van den Borne's potato farm is at the center of the digital agriculture revolution. And it is farms like Van den Borne's that are poised to help feed and nourish our world by 2050.

A BROKEN FOOD SYSTEM

By 2050, the world's population is projected to reach 9.8 billion.[4] Nearly all of this population increase will come from developing countries. Urbanization, especially in India, China, and Nigeria, will continue at an accelerated pace, and nearly 70% of the world's population will be urban by 2050 (compared to 55% in 2018).[5]

In order to sufficiently feed this large, urban population, the UN Food and Agriculture Organization (FAO) estimates that food production will need to increase by 70% from 2005 to 2050.[6] Alarmingly, 2017 saw a continued increase in global hunger levels; nearly 821 million people are on the brink of starvation with insufficient food to lead a healthy, active life.[7] That's one in nine people and 11% of the world's population in 2018.[8] Of the 821 million people, 98%, live in developing countries, with the highest rates seen in Asia and Sub-Saharan Africa.[9] Rather ironically, 50% of the world's hungry people are from farming families, with resource-poor smallholder farmers being the natural victims.[10]

The challenge of trying to feed a growing population doesn't always reveal the entire picture of the global hunger problem. A large part of the global hunger problem is not merely calorific hunger, it's also nutrient hunger, or malnutrition. Feeding the world enough calorically is one thing, but feeding the world nutritionally well is a whole new ball game. About 2 billion people worldwide do not get enough essential vitamins and minerals in their diets.[14] In children under 5 years of age, around 45% of deaths are linked to under nutrition.[15] We need to feed people food that helps them maintain a healthy and nutritionally balanced lifestyle. In other words, we must nourish people, not just feed them.

I'm not the first and certainly not the last person to tell you that eradicating hunger and malnutrition is one of the greatest challenges and missions of humankind. Not only do the consequences of insufficient food cause suffering and poor health, they also hinder progress in important areas of development like education, income inequality, and employment.

If we're unable to feed and nourish the world today, how are we possibly going to feed millions more mouths by 2050? The great paradox is that we already produce enough food to feed our current population.[11] Of course, we waste a third of it (1.3 billion tonnes annually[12]). We use a large bulk of it to produce biofuels and animal feed, rather than food for the almost 1 billion hungry. And the people making less than US$2 a day? They can't afford to buy this food.[13]

Invariably, hunger is caused by poverty, inequality, and inefficiency throughout the supply chain. In reality, the urgent call to rapidly increase food production by 2050 only applies if we continue to inefficiently produce and distribute food and prioritize livestock and fuel production over hungry people.

Severe weather fluctuations, economic slowdowns, political instability, and the increasing scarcity of key resources —land, water, energy—have and will continue to pose great challenges for global food production. In particular, the impacts of climate change will be felt significantly by the agriculture sector. A warming climate could cut global crop yields by more than 25%.[14] By 2050, extreme weather events, unpredictable changes in precipitation, rising sea levels, and the increase in pest and disease damage will undoubtedly have devastating effects on farmers, land, and crops.

At the same time, unsustainable food production is putting immense strain on our environment. While agriculture is affected by climate change, it also significantly contributes to it. The global agri-food sector is currently the second highest source of carbon emissions (behind the energy sector),[15] contributing up to 29% of global greenhouse gas emissions.[16] Unsurprisingly, the meat and dairy industry are massive culprits, contributing a whopping 60% of total agricultural greenhouse gas emissions.[17] In fact, the world's top five meat and dairy companies are already collectively responsible for more annual greenhouse gas emissions than Exxon Mobile, Shell, or BP.[18] That's absolutely shocking.

Considering this, the meat and dairy industry is already on track to become the world's biggest contributors to climate change in the next decade.[19] The continuation of current livestock sector practices could make the sector solely responsible for 80% of the allowable greenhouse gas budget by 2050,[20] severely inhibiting our ability to meet the 2015 Paris UN Climate Change Agreement's goal of limiting global temperature increase to 1.5°C above pre-industrial levels.[21]

Another often-overlooked area is the impact of food waste on the climate. The 30% of food wasted globally across the food supply chain contributes a significant 8% of global greenhouse gas emissions.[22] If food waste were a country, it would be the third largest greenhouse gas emitting country in the world, after the United States and China.[23] If we redirected food waste to feed hungry people, we could both offset its significant carbon emissions and alleviate global hunger. Essentially, we'd kill two birds with one stone.

Despite agriculture's critical role in future emissions, action and climate financing to reduce emissions from this sector has traditionally lagged behind other sectors, with an overwhelming focus by policymakers and climate advocates on the energy sector. However, considering its significant contributions to global warming, food and agriculture must be a larger part of the climate discussion. In fact, a recent ranking by Project Drawdown of the top solutions to combat global warming showed that of the top 20 solutions, eight relate to the food system, while only five have to do with electricity generation.[24] In the coming decades, will we effectively prioritize our efforts in the fight against global warming?

Our current food system is inherently broken, inefficient, inequitable, and highly unsustainable. The agriculture industry undoubtedly has a far-reaching impact and the need for food systems that meet the needs of the farmer, consumer, and the planet has never been greater.

If we are to nourish 821 million people who are hungry today and 2 billion more people expected to be undernourished by 2050, a profound change in the global agri-food system needs to happen. If we are to meet the United Nations Sustainable Development Goal Number Two of Zero Hunger by 2030,[25] we're going to need to wake up to the deep-seated and institutional flaws of our global food system.

In our resource constraint yet resource consumption-heavy world, a true revolution in farming and the global food system is urgently needed. I believe that revolution begins and ends with technological and digital transformation. Rapid advances in technological innovation will allow us to reimagine and re-shape the entire food system, helping us find solutions to our most pressing food production problems. Without a doubt, food is hungry for disruption.

A BRIEF HISTORY OF FOOD AND AGRICULTURE

To understand where food and agriculture is heading in the future, we must understand its history. It all started way back in 10,000 BC with the First Agricultural Revolution, or commonly known as the Neolithic Revolution.[26] At the very core of this period was the pre-historic transition from a lifestyle of hunting and gathering to settled agriculture, allowing for a larger population to exist. Humans learned how plants grew and developed, and soon domesticated them into crop cultivation.

Between the 8th century and the 18th century, farming tools basically stayed the same with few advancements in technology.[27] Things really started to radically change in the 18th century with the arrival of the Second Agricultural Revolution, a period of agricultural development that saw a massive increase in agricultural productivity and vast improvements in farm technology.[28]

During the Second Agricultural Revolution, agricultural mechanization and commercialization enabled unprecedented increases in land and labor productivity. The plow and seed drill became critical farm tools that reduced the need for seeding and plowing by hand. Horse-drawn mechanical reapers soon replaced the sickle, the curved tool used by humans to harvest grain crops. Reapers were then replaced by reaper binders, which were in turn replaced by the combine harvester.[29] Ultimately, the revolution saw the increasing use of machinery marking the pivotal shift from hand power to horsepower and finally, to machine power.

At the same time, the food canning industry, one of the first major food preservation techniques, was established, forever changing food production and consumption. The steamboat and the railroad enabled mass transportation of both people and food across oceans, expanding food distribution beyond borders.[30] While not a new technique, crossbreeding developed immensely. Farmers and scientists crossbred plants within a species, selecting plant genes for the most desirable traits.

By the 1950s, tractors soon replaced horses, which meant that land used to grow oats and hay for horses could be used for greater mass production of corn and soy.[31] Mechanical harvesters, seeders, and plows were prevalent. Combine harvesters pretty much replaced the reaper binder. Cows started being machine milked. Soon, the Green Revolution, or the Third Agricultural Revolution, emerged.

From the 1950s to the late 1970s, the Green Revolution brought on a whole host of new technologies that radically accelerated another wave of agricultural productivity. The development of high-yielding varieties of cereals, the use of chemical fertilizers, and the modernization of farm management techniques all greatly increased global food production.[32] During this time, food productivity gains were unprecedented; between 1950 and 1984, world grain production increased by a whopping 160%.[33] Evidently, the advancements made during this period completely transformed global food production and helped feed billions of hungry people.

However, while the production increases of the Green Revolution helped avoid mass famine, it all came at an incredible cost to the environment. With the heavy reliance on agrochemicals and machines, agriculture became increasingly reliant on crude oil extraction and greatly increased greenhouse gas emissions.[34] The heavy overuse of agrochemicals also caused major problems like land degradation, nutrient overrun in groundwater systems, the loss of biodiversity, and the exploitation of grazing land and fisheries.[35] Again, agriculture is both a victim and a culprit of climate change.

Beyond damages to the environment, the Green Revolution severely damaged the quality of food produced, and therefore our diets. Rather than incorporating polycultures as in traditional agriculture, the revolution overwhelmingly focused on the monoculture farming of cereal grains. This led to the overproduction of cheap grain, which ultimately fueled the emergence of highly processed foods with little nutritional quality. With its cheapness and addictiveness, junk foods like chips, soda, and burgers flew off supermarket shelves and out drive-thru windows, marking the mass consumption of these foods. The rise of monocultures ultimately drove highly processed junk foods into the mainstream.

My grandmother, a baby boomer who grew up in the mid 1940s to the 1960s, has an intense liking for potato chips and junk food in general. To this day, she usually has a bag of Ruffles Sour Cream and Onion potato chips in her bedroom ready for her midnight snack. Needless to say, she can't quite get over the addictive crunch and taste of them. My grandma is a testament to how foods like Pringles are engineered to make you eat 20 more chips after you have had 30. Undoubtedly, the addictiveness of such foods came at the detriment of the health of humans and brought about the horrific rise of diet-related diseases like diabetes and heart disease that we see today.

So, while monoculture farming during the Green Revolution was successful in increasing grain yields and reducing hunger, it significantly degraded the nutritional quality of our diets. In essence, it failed to focus food production on a healthy diet. It was great at feeding people calorically, but not so much at feeding people nutritionally well. Unfortunately, the Green Revolution left greater problems for the future to solve.

FOOD AND AGRICULTURE TODAY

Today, food is still engineered to be tasty and addictive, with the mass production of commodity crops like corn, wheat, and soy fueling the highly processed junk food industry.

However, recent calls for a greater focus on health and nutrition in the food community is quickly improving and enhancing the quality of our diets.

Currently, conventional and selective breeding methods are still being deployed to produce crops with highly attractive characteristics like disease resistance. An example close to home is the conventional breeding research being done at a tissue culture lab near my childhood home in Malaysia. Since my family comes from the palm oil business, I visited one of our palm oil estates when I was 13. Palm trees towered tall above me and I saw how incredibly cumbersome it was to harvest palm fruit bunches with a 6-feet-long sickle.

Naturally, everyone in the business is trying to breed shorter and more accessible-to-harvest trees. That lab near my home was doing the same. Behind those lab doors, researchers were breeding palm tree seedlings and selecting for specific traits. Desirable traits such as a high oil-to-fruit ratio, shorter height palms, and resistance to a deadly root disease called Ganoderma Basal Stem Rot (BSR), were all crucial to the productivity and profitability of my family's business.[36] Today, conventional and selective breeding techniques are equally prevalent in other commodity crops like soybeans and potatoes.

In stark contrast, genetically modified organisms (GMOs) have a bad reputation amongst consumers and face major scrutiny despite helping to make large strides in genetic crop improvement. However, whether through conventional and selective breeding or genetic modification, every commercially available vegetable, fruit, and grain has been altered by human hands, even those coming from organic and heirloom seeds. The non-GMO labels you see are wildly deceiving.

Today, our food distribution systems are highly inefficient; such systems are the root of our high hunger and malnutrition rates. If inefficiency alone wasn't bad enough, the food supply chain has one of the heaviest carbon footprints. This is mostly due to the ridiculous miles our food travels and energy-sucking cold supply chains. Specifically, it is due to our expectations of the fresh and often non-locally produced foods in our supermarkets. Ever had a strawberry during the winter? I've got news for you: Strawberries don't grow in the winter where you are. Plus, they certainly don't come from anywhere near where you are. How did it get to you?

Today, the average farm still looks like the farm you'd see during the years of the Green Revolution. A mid-to-large size farm still uses tractors and combines to plow, seed, fertilize, and harvest fields. However, the development of embedded sensors, network infrastructure, and data analytics have allowed larger farms to become more digital savvy. Despite some digitization, not all farms are as connected or analytics-driven as you think. Most farms are still old school, using legacy systems that collect data only to be kept in data warehouses for months on end and not shared across the Cloud. Utilization of that data is also limited, with many farmers questioning the larger uses of their data. Surprisingly or unsurprisingly, farms today don't yet have the level of digitization that industries like the media or mining has experienced.

Our current food and agricultural system is far from perfect. The challenges we face today will evolve into new challenges that require a completely new set of solutions in the future. Our global food system will simply have to change for the better.

HUNGRY FOR DISRUPTION

By 2050, our food and agricultural system will look drastically different than it does today—and more like the work Jacob Van den Borne is pioneering on his 550-hectare potato farm in the Netherlands. Van den Borne, the "Pope of Precision Agriculture," has seen and shown firsthand how technology can revolutionize the farm. By embracing the use of smart data and autonomous systems, he easily operates the most productive potato farm in the world.

In the coming decades, we're going to need to embrace technological innovation like Van den Borne has. Food production in the 21st century is facing multiple challenges: it has to produce more nutritious food to feed a growing population with a smaller rural labor force, adopt more efficient and sustainable production methods amidst increasing scarcity of resources, adapt to climate change, and in turn reduce its impact on climate change.[37]

Humankind is facing unprecedented challenges in food production, but the food and agriculture technologies explored in this book has made me as optimistic as ever about the future of nourishing our world by 2050. Because while we live in a world of significant challenges, we also live in one where the pace of scientific and technological advances is unparalleled.

In 2050, our food and agricultural system will be driven by technological innovations that help us meet our global food and health demands, all whilst minimizing our resource use. Innovations in precision agriculture, indoor farming, genomics, alternative protein, and technologies that improve food safety and reduce food waste will play an enormous role in enhancing the agri-food systems of our future. These breakthrough innovations will dramatically accelerate the efficiency and productivity of our farms and provide us with wildly novel ways of producing our food. It will also change what we eat in the coming decades.

While technology is not the entire solution to the global hunger problem, it is certainly a critical component. Without the forces of science and technology-based solutions, the world's potential to face the aforementioned challenges is bleak. In the coming decades, the adoption of these technological innovations will improve global nutrition, promote environmental sustainability, and contribute to pressing areas of development like poverty and inequality.

The future of food is fast, fresh, and hungry for disruption, requiring new solutions to a completely new set of challenges. While no one is omniscient, one thing I am certain about is that rapid technological advancements will cause the food industry to change more in the next 10 years than it has in the last 30. This book explores those drastic changes in our food system and paints a vision of how technological innovations can better our food system by 2050.

The chapters in this book are built around 4 parts. Part 1, "The Digitization and Automation of Farms," examines how the Internet of Things (IoT), artificial intelligence, and autonomous systems like robots and drones will revolutionize the farm. Part 2, "Novel Farming Systems," explores how indoor farming technologies and smart home micro-gardens will radically change the current framework of field farming and make food production more accessible, efficient, and productive than ever. Part 3, "Re-engineering Our Food," is really all about how advancements in genomics and food science have allowed us to make the shift from engineering food to taste better to re-engineering food to actually be better for us and the planet. Finally, part 4, "Streamlining the Global Food Supply Chain," dives deeper into technologies that reduce food waste and increase transparency throughout the global food supply chain.

These four parts comprise of areas where innovations like robotics, aquaponics, cell-cultured meat, gene editing, and the blockchain are poised to disrupt the future of food and agriculture. Through its exploration of breakthrough technologies, this book is a read for agri-food businesses and entrepreneurs looking to explore and expand the notion of what it will mean to produce and distribute food in the coming decades. More specifically, it aims to help those in the industry be cognizant of the technologies that will disrupt the US$7.8 trillion global food and agriculture industry.[38]

More broadly and importantly, it is for the everyday consumer to educate themselves about where their food comes from and where it will come from in the next decades. Rarely do we stop and think about where our food comes from, who produced it, how they produced it, or how it got to you. However, I can't make a bigger case for food.

Food is at the nexus of almost all of our world's most pressing social issues—hunger, poverty, global health, education, unemployment, inequality, global warming. Food plays an integral role in all of our lives. It brings us joy and nourishment. It transcends cultural and political barriers. It enhances the relationship between man and nature. But it is also the root of pressing global issues like diet-related diseases and climate change.

Considering the wide-reaching impacts of our global food system, consumers like you and I must educate ourselves and do our part. The decisions we make every day regarding the food we purchase and consume is perhaps the single most important contribution we can make to reducing global warming and building a better food system for the world.

For the benefit of humanity, the global food system must change for the better. The adoption of the technological innovations explored in this book will be critical forces that drive the future of a more sustainable, inclusive, and delicious tomorrow.

PART I

THE DIGITIZATION AND AUTOMATION OF FARMS

CHAPTER 1

THE AGE OF SMART AGRICULTURE

———

Welcome to the future of smart agriculture, where the Internet of Things (IoT), data analytics, and artificial intelligence (AI) are empowering farmers to build the most efficient and sustainable food systems the world has ever seen.

"Software is eating the world."[1]

Marc Andreessen, co-founder and general partner of venture capital firm Andreessen Horowitz, famously said these words. His highly quoted phrase is made clear by just looking to the likes of companies like ride-sharing giant Uber and online payments decacorn Stripe and their sky-high valuations.

Kirk Haney, managing director of food and agriculture technology venture capital firm Radicle Growth, elaborates on that statement.

"Software is eating the connected world. The farm is not yet connected," Haney tells me.[2]

As the managing director of one of the U.S.'s few food and agriculture tech focused venture funds, Haney has good reason to know. Agriculture is one of the least digitized sectors; the lack of IT infrastructure in agriculture opens up massive opportunities to create new connected systems and tap into a US$7.8 trillion global agri-food industry.[3]

In the '90s, wireless internet technology completely changed the trajectory of enterprise software and created connected devices like Smartphones. Information and data became readily available across any internet-connected device, making it easy to access information and derive data insights. However, the farm doesn't yet have that level of connectivity. It is hungry for that level of connectivity.

How do we connect the farmer to the farm just as Google connected us to the rest of the world? How do we easily equip farmers with the information they need to make informed decisions?

With challenges, come opportunity. From 2019 to 2025, the number of connected devices is going to grow from an estimated 19 billion to 34 billion.[4] That is a tremendous opportunity for the digitization of farms.

From supply chain to books, every industry is experiencing digital transformation. Agriculture is no different. In the next 30 years, we'll build connected and smart farms that optimize farm management like never before. In the next 30 years, we'll use the power of artificial intelligence (AI) and predictive modeling to make smart data work for the farmer and create greater transparency in our agricultural markets.

THE 21ST CENTURY FARMER

Keith Gingerich is a third-generation farmer and the operations manager at Gingerich Farms, a successful family farm with 10,000 acres of corn, soybean, and wheat in East-Central Illinois.[5] While you'd probably imagine his day to day involves plowing fields or soil sampling, his job actually looks more like a technician's or a farm data analyst's.

He spends a lot of time in his high-tech tractor-meets-office, fully equipped with screens and control panels of different systems. He views and analyzes data about his entire farm, using the valuable insights generated to optimize his input usage and increase yields.[6]

Remote sensors monitor moisture and nitrogen levels in fields miles away. Yield analysis tools recommend underperforming areas that require more attention. A weather feature advises whether fields are workable based on historical and current conditions. Drones fly around and survey the field, providing high-resolution images and data that reveal information about the farm that Gingerich would only see if he physically stepped foot on the farm at a later date.

Without going out and surveying each field, Gingerich and other farmers at Gingerich Farms can access quality field and yield performance data with a touch of a phone or computer tablet. Basically, he can find out everything he needs to know about his farm's conditions without even stepping foot on his farm. Now that's what I call a smart farm. Keith Gingerich is the definition of a 21st century farmer embracing digital agriculture. If we'll need to produce more nutritious food amidst a highly unpredictable and resource-scarce future, we'll need more farmers like Keith.

A CONNECTED FARM

In the past, farmers have relied primarily on experience and instinct to manage their farm. A traditional, disconnected farm is one where farmers manually collect data about their farm through physically surveying the field. For instance, for farmers to test the pH and salinity of soil, he or she would have to spend several hours physically collecting soil samples and conducting tests on each soil sample.

They'd likely store this data in some sort of database application or Excel spreadsheet, or perhaps even on plain ol' pen and paper. Analyzing historical data would look something like using mere instinct and observation or manually generating graphs and/or tables to illustrate key trends. The problem is that data is discrete and not updated in real time, rather than continuous and frequently updated.

In contrast, a connected farm looks and operates very differently. The key component of any smart, connected farm is the agricultural Internet of Things (IoT), which consists of the collection of data from digital devices like sensors with the ability for farmers to view and interact with this data on digital platforms. For instance, a connected farm would have sensors installed in the field that transmit real-time field data to the Cloud and to connected devices like a tablet. This allows the farmer to gather and analyze data about the field's water levels, soil conditions, weather, air quality, and disease in each section of the farm from his/her computer and phone. Essentially, the agricultural IoT connects the farmer to data about his/her farm.

Not only can the farmer view this real-time data on a digital platform, most IoT platforms provide a higher level of data analysis, combining this historical data with GPS and satellite weather models to predict future growing conditions and provide specific recommendations to the farmer.

Keith Gingerich describes what big data has and will do for farmers all over the world:

"We are seeing the same acres, but we now have sensors, controllers, and software that give us a HD look at what was always stored in our minds through observations. Now the equipment tells what we will see later before we can see it now."[7]

That is what a connected farm does—digitizing a farmer's observations highly efficiently and quickly without manual data entry. These "digitized observations" suddenly become something that is not just stored in a farmers' mind, but can be manipulated and analyzed using digital tools in order to generate useful information to optimize farm management operations. Armed with this valuable information, farmers can make smarter decisions and make their farms significantly more efficient and dynamic.

The current lack of digitization on farms means we still have progress to make before smart, connected farms become ubiquitous. However, rapid advancements in IoT infrastructure and the plummeting costs of sensors and data storage are paving the way for smart agriculture to take the industry by storm. Digital tools like smart irrigation systems and drones will increasingly arm farmers with real-time field data to make better agronomic decisions. Such digital tools are already enhancing the most digital savvy farms, and are poised to continue to disrupt the farming industry.

THE BILLION DOLLAR OPPORTUNITY

Today, we have smartphones and smartwatches. By 2050, futurists predict we will have smart homes. But what about smart farms?

The founders of The Climate Corporation believe in the future of smart farms.

Originally founded in 2006 by two former Google employees, The Climate Corporation is a digital agriculture company that provides weather, soil, and field data to help farmers optimize yield and maximize profit. It aims to take the guesswork out of issues like weather and crop disease and uses its real-time data to underwrite weather insurance for farmers.[8]

The Climate Corporation's main product, the Climate Fieldview platform, helps farmers collect, store, and visualize critical field data. Farmers then use these data insights to monitor the impact of agronomic decisions on crop performance, evaluate yield productivity, and manage crop risk. In fact, Keith Gingerich, the aforementioned farmer from Illinois, saw an 11% yield boost on Gingerich Farms since using Climate Corporation's technology.[9] That's how much more productive such digital solutions make the farm.

The Climate Corporation has a bold mission—to help all the world's farmers sustainably increase productivity with digital tools.[10] In 2013, Monsanto believed in The Climate Corporation's mission enough to acquire the startup for US$930 million.[11]

The almost US$1 billion acquisition combined The Climate Corporation's expertise in agriculture analytics and risk-management with Monsanto's R&D and biotech capabilities, providing farmers with a comprehensive picture of all the factors that affect the success of their crops. The companies' combined capabilities will support greater productivity while using the planet's finite resources more precisely.

Ultimately, the acquisition marked the urgent need and potential for greater productivity on the farm. Monsanto estimated that "the majority of farmers have an untapped yield opportunity of up to 30 bushels to 50 bushels in their corn fields... advancements in data science can help further unlock that additional value for the farm."[12] In fact, it is theoretically possible to harvest 530 bushels of corn per acre, but the U.S. average is only 168 bushels.[13] That's some wasted potential output right there.

David Friedberg, founder of The Climate Corporation, identified this untapped opportunity early on:

"Farmers around the world are challenged to make key decisions for their farms in the face of increasingly volatile weather, as well as a proliferation of information sources...the ability to turn data into actionable insight and farm management recommendations is vitally important for agriculture around the world and can greatly benefit farmers, regardless of farm size or their preferred farming methods."[14]

In the coming decades, digital tools and software like the Climate Fieldview will make farmers incredibly effective in optimizing yield with precise uses of agricultural inputs like fertilizers. The digitization of farms to create smart agriculture will radically disrupt the way farmers currently operate; in the process, it will create the most productive farms agriculture has ever seen.

PRECISE AGRICULTURE

"Optimizing the usage of our resources and sustainability is synonymous with precision. Sustainability simply must be precise."[15]

Michael Eaton, founder of micro-hydroponic growing system startup Iko Systems, tells me as we discuss how sustainable agriculture is today and the future of farming.

Michael understands the intense need for precision in farming. He grew up in Botswana, a country, much like many others, where agriculture is vitally important for the livelihood of its population. However, the challenge for Botswana is its lack of key resources and unsuitable climate for crops to thrive. The country's highly variable rainfall coupled by the fact that desert and poor soils cover 70% of the country, makes Botswana incredibly limited in agricultural productivity.[16]

Michael has seen firsthand what being precise in terms of water and fertilizer usage means for optimizing production yields in a resource-scarce nation like Botswana. His country depends on optimizing its use of scarce resources to provide enough food for its country and maintain the livelihood of Botswanan farmers.

In the coming decades, more and more countries will start experiencing conditions and climates as unsuitable for agriculture as Botswana's. Drought-prone countries like Chile, Namibia, and Israel are already on track to be incredibly water stressed by 2050.[17] To maintain agricultural productivity in these regions, precision and optimization of resources will become critically crucial in order to sufficiently nourish the world. This need for greater optimization has brought about the emergence of precision agriculture, which involves the use of information technologies and devices like sensors and robots in order to make more precise agronomic decisions.

Precision agriculture isn't a new concept. The first waves of precision agriculture came about with the introduction of GPS guidance for tractors in the early 1990s; the adoption of this technology is now the most commonly used example of precision agriculture today.[18] John Deere, the farm management and equipment company, was one of the pioneers of using GPS location data from satellites. It works by having a GPS-connected tractor automatically steer the tractor based on field coordinates. This allowed drivers to reduce steering errors as well as overlap passes on the field. As a result, there was less wasted seed, fertilizer, fuel, and time.[19]

The integration of GPS and geographic information systems (GIS) spearheaded the rise of agricultural mechanization in the 1990s. Since then, precision agriculture has developed tremendously. The rapid advancement of information technologies has transformed precision agriculture from standard monitoring using satellite imaging and geographic sensing to more specific and controlled monitoring using in-field sensing technologies. This has allowed farmers to make the revolutionary shift from broad, field-wide decision making to more plant specific decision-making—a major key in the complex science of maintaining hectares upon hectares of crops while dealing with individual plants that require different levels of treatment.

Think of it as a company's marketing spend. Marketers—decent ones at least—don't just pump money into every channel possible. They first evaluate which channels provide them with the highest impressions, clicks, or leads per dollar spent. Then, they use those intelligent insights to allocate their marketing spend accordingly, ensuring they get the most value out of their buck.

Similarly, the farmer aims to minimize the amount of farm inputs like water or fertilizer required to maintain a healthy crop. A prime example of a precision agriculture tool is in Variable Rate Technology (VRT). VRT involves the use of autonomous vehicles to apply variable amounts of inputs in specific areas according to data on how much each plant needs. By optimizing inputs, considerable costs and negative impacts like nutrient runoff are reduced. This is especially crucial for the livelihoods of farmers, since the majority of a farmer's costs are in his/her inputs, assuming the land is not considered.

The emergence of better precision agriculture has brought about an entirely new meaning for digital agriculture. Instead of just managing and monitoring field and plant-related data, precision agriculture takes it a step further by intelligently analyzing that data and using the derived insights to inform autonomous tools like robots how to maintain and optimize the farm. We'll discuss more about agricultural robots in Chapter 2 and drones in Chapter 3.

With advanced precision agriculture techniques, farmers can ensure greater profitability, efficiency, and sustainability in optimizing their resource usage. While precision agriculture principles have been around for about 30 years, recent technological advancements like the use of AI in yield prediction have greatly enhanced precision agriculture practices. The potent combination of the rapid adoption of connected mobile devices, better access to low-cost sensors and high-speed wireless networks, and sophisticated AI will pave the path for precision agriculture to become the norm in smart farming by 2050.

DIGITAL AGRICULTURE FOR SMALLHOLDERS

One of the core criticisms and challenges of big data systems and precision agriculture is that these tools aren't easily accessible nor applicable to smallholder farmers in developing nations. However, tools like Microsoft's AI Sowing App are changing that paradigm.

In a pilot program with 175 farmers in the state of Andhra Pradesh, India in 2016, Microsoft's AI Sowing app allowed farmers to achieve an average of 30% higher yields per hectare compared to the previous year.[20] The AI Sowing App, powered by Microsoft Cortana Intelligence Suite, is the result of collaboration between Microsoft and the International Crop Research Institute for the Semi-Arid Tropics

(ICRISAT).[21] At its core, the app sends sowing advisories to participating farmers regarding the optimal date to sow.

To predict the optimal crop-sowing period, historical climate and rainfall data from the last 30 years was analyzed using AI. The data was used to create weather forecasting models that provided predictability, allowing the system to guide farmers regarding the ideal sowing week via text messages.[22]

The reason that the AI sowing app is making such information systems accessible to smallholder farmers is that the app requires minimal infrastructure on the farmers' part - there is no need to install any sensors in their fields nor incur any capital expenditure. All farmers need is a phone capable of receiving text messages about optimal sowing dates, land preparation, and soil test-based fertilizer application.[23] The app is exemplary of how we can leverage the high mobile penetration of developing nations like India in order to build Smartphone-based solutions that are highly accessible to the small-to-medium farmer.

Joseph Shen, founder of AI-driven crop analysis mobile app RiseHarvest that works with farmers in Myanmar, tells me his hope for Smartphone-based solutions in developing nations:

"I'd like to see it [AI-based Smartphone solutions] proliferating and leveling the plane field. I think the great power of Smartphone solutions is it gives poorer farmers in places like Myanmar the same access to knowledge as the most sophisticated farmer in Australia or in any other developed country."[24]

Increasing smallholder farmers' access to these digital tools is vitally important not only for greater equality in the agricultural system, but also because smallholder farmers play a critical role in countries in Africa and Asia—80% of the farmland in sub-Saharan Africa and Asia is managed by smallholders (working on up to 10 hectares).[25] Smallholders are crucial for the livelihoods and food sufficiency of these nations.

A key direction to build solutions that are accessible to smallholders is to scale down information technologies and lower the barriers of entry to using these systems. Currently, there are two main barriers:

1. The high upfront capital costs of using these connected systems and software
2. The lack of network infrastructure to use these connected systems in these developing nations

The first barrier, cost, will decrease over time. Like many new technologies such as robotics and drones, savings in optimized resources and additional value in maximized output will offset the high upfront capital costs. And as the cost of sensors and storing data in the Cloud drops, these connected systems will soon become more financially accessible to farmers.

The second barrier, network infrastructure, is a more complicated one. Wireless, high-speed internet and robust computing power is becoming increasingly accessible and cheaper in developing nations. However, the problem is that smallholder farmers don't operate large farms and sophisticated enterprise software systems are often synonymous with only being applicable to large businesses. A way to tackle this is to build scaled-down solutions that do not require as much infrastructure. Low-infrastructure solutions like Microsoft's AI Sowing app will continue to ensure that small-to-medium farmers can also adopt these digital tools for their benefit.

However, the question of whether these farm management software systems would even be compatible or valuable for these smallholder farms is questionable—would these small farms even produce enough data for something like a yield prediction tool to be credible? That's a question that tools like Microsoft's AI Sowing app is demystifying.

While developing countries currently suffer from a lack of farm digitization and modernization, there is no question that smallholder farmers in these areas desperately need these solutions. More often than not, these farmers rely on agriculture for their livelihoods and it definitely isn't an easy business.

Adverse weather, scarce resources, and high costs all become debilitating challenges for the smallholder farmer. Yet, if we can provide mobile-first digital solutions like Rise-Harvest's crop analysis app to farmers, we can help make them smarter in using their scarce resources to achieve incredible levels of output. With this, we can only hope that a country like India, responsible for almost 25% of the world's hungry, can be better equipped to feed the estimated

196 million people that go hungry every year in the country.[26] Alec Ross, author of *Industries of the Future*, shares the same hope:

"The best hope for India is that precision agriculture provides a leapfrog opportunity, helping its subsistence-level farmers achieve a level of performance that is impossible for them today. It represents the best hope for feeding the hundreds of millions of people in India who don't have enough to eat today."[27]

In adopting more accessible precision agriculture tools in the future, the power of big data will proliferate and level the playing field between small and large farms. These solutions will serve to feed farmers hungry for data-driven insights, enabling every farmer to produce greater efficiency yields to nourish the world by 2050.

THE AFRICAN DROUGHT CRISIS: TURNING BIG DATA INTO SMART DATA

It was May 2016 and the city of Cape Town, South Africa was on the verge of becoming the first major urban center to run out of water.[28] Scorched rocks, the dilapidated remains of long dead trees, ruins of hot white sand, and dried-up rows of Chenin Blanc vines covered the town. Cape Town looked like a scene right out of the Sahara Desert. It was the advent of the great drought that would continue indefinitely.

Producing enough food to sustain Cape Town's population was a major issue and limiting exports to maintain minimum food supply levels was high on the government's priority agenda. Not to mention the challenges the wine industry would face in exporting 449 million liters of wine in 2017.[29] The thought of all that lost South African Sauvignon Blanc and Chenin Blanc was almost too hard to bear for the rest of the world.

Fast forward to 2018 and Theewaterskloof, the biggest reservoir in Cape Town, is a diminished pool after three years of relentless drought that has reduced it to barely a tenth of its 480-billion-liter capacity.[30] Cape Town has managed to momentarily avert the crisis. Day Zero, the doomsday moment when municipal government would have to turn off taps and force citizens to queue at security-guarded water pipes, has been pushed back indefinitely.

Key word—*indefinitely*. Dominique Sian Doyle, former Energy Policy Officer of Earthlife Africa Johannesburg, tells me what it's really like to live in these dire conditions:

"Day Zero as we call it is 2 days away. Already, one side of town has been without water for 3 days. The people there are very poor, with an unemployment rate of 70%. They cannot afford to fetch or buy water. It's a giant scary mess. Our municipality is so dysfunctional that it has not been managing the problem. Our town is kind of in the middle of nowhere in a rural province of South Africa, so I am not sure how we are going to get water in.

It's really interesting to see how the town continues to wait till the last minute to start saving water. Still toilets are being

flushed, baths are being taken, swimming pools filled. Some-
times I think the only way humanity will learn is the hard way.
And shit is about to get very real in this town."[31]

Drought is one of the major constraints affecting food
security and livelihoods of more than two billion people.[32]
Severe droughts in water-stressed places like California, South
Africa, and Israel have drastically affected agricultural productivity and food production. Soon enough, Day Zero will
loom over more countries. How is the world going to cope?

Beyond precision agriculture, the use of big data in predictive analytics and forecast modeling is spearheading the
arrival of smart data in agriculture. Smart data that will allow
us to mitigate the risks of weather adversities like droughts
and floods that deeply affect food production. Smart data
that will allow us to have greater predictability and certainty
in volatile agricultural markets.

The interdependence and interconnectivity of global
agriculture makes it a highly complex market that is hard to
navigate. Forecasting the conditions of global agriculture, like
predicting a drought or its impact on crop yields, involves
complex modeling using highly relevant data. Currently, predictions about things like crop yield and price are often made
based on ad hoc intuition using hard-to-acquire data.

In the case of South Africa, merely understanding how the
drought will affect the country's production yields is not enough
to avert the crisis. Understanding the risks of limiting exports to
external countries is also critical. On one hand, taking measures

to limit exports would help maintain minimum supply levels to sustain Cape Town's population. On the other hand, limiting exports too much may hurt the livelihoods of agricultural producers reliant on international exports and possibly even hurt relationships with exporting countries.

That's where the next generation of big data startups like Gro Intelligence can add immense value.

Gro Intelligence, a global agriculture data analytics company, collects and synthesizes trillions of data points about supply, demand, weather, and environment data from disparate and often previously unavailable sources in the global agriculture industry.[33] Beyond aggregating data, Gro develops analytical tools and predictive models that combine domain expertise with machine learning to provide users with current and future insights into the global food and agriculture industry.[34]

Big data analytics platforms like Gro's will help all agricultural stakeholders use data-driven models to make highly informed decisions and mitigate an impending crisis. For instance, a drought indicator using predictive models is able to present information like current and predicted drought conditions, which crops are most impacted, how much to limit exports, and how the drought would affect future growing seasons.

"The challenge [in agriculture] now is to convert big data into smart data," says Barak Cohen, product manager at Gro Intelligence.[35]

With the buzz surrounding big data, tons of data is being generated and stored. Nevertheless, data alone isn't useful if it isn't converted and manipulated into information and insights. The future lies in building tools such as Gro's forecast models that make data derived insights available in a very accessible form.

Beyond predicting a drought, we'll soon be able to detect famines faster and more efficiently than we currently do. With a deep understanding of the complex agricultural market coupled with strong forecast models, we can eventually predict a food shortage before it even happens. This means that countries can put in place preventative measures like increasing food imports to ensure that a country's future food supply is not severely harmed. By doing so, we can mitigate a future food crisis due to disruptions to agriculture.

With the tremendous advancement of big data analytics and machine learning capabilities, we'll soon be able to detect agriculture-damaging crises like droughts more accurately and efficiently than we've ever done. By 2050, big data and predictive analytics will play a central role in helping countries like South Africa mitigate severe weather and food crises.

TRANSPARENCY AND DATA DEMOCRATIZATION

The World Bank Food Price Index rose by 43% between June 2010 and January 2011, reaching its highest levels since 1990 in February 2011.[36] That was a scary time in the food world.

Though contentious, the 2010-2012 world food price spike crisis was partly due to the perceived, not actual, fall in grain stocks.

The 2010-2012 spike was triggered by severe heat waves in Russia, which forecasted a 30% reduction in wheat harvests, triggering a major export ban.[37] Despite this, writers in major publications like *The Economist* and *The Financial Times* claimed that there was enough wheat in stock and "prices are unlikely to surge to the all-time highs of 2007-2008."[38] Other news stories that highlighted locust outbreaks in Australia and heavy rains in Canada further served to increase the perception of an impending grain shortage.

Naturally, upon hearing Russia's forecasts, Egypt and other North African states bought and imported an excessive amount of grain stocks, leading to the global increase of grain prices.[39] In just one month (June-July 2010), the price of maize and wheat each rose by a whopping 25%.[40] Ultimately, large-scale imports of agricultural commodities in 2011 triggered the global food price spike.

In the case of the 2010-2011 food price spike, the perceived and highly exaggerated grain shortage triggered the market to experience price spikes that exceeded the price levels seen in 2007-2008. All this had a cascading effect and resulted in price hikes in other staples like cocoa and rubber. Clearly, the lack of data accessibility in agricultural markets makes room for asymmetric information (when market participants do not have identical information to make key decisions). As microeconomic principles dictate, imperfect markets eventually lead to inefficient outcomes.

Ultimately, agricultural markets with imperfect information will lead to crises such as the 2010-2011 price hikes. In order for efficient commodity trading and decision-making to occur, every stakeholder in our food and agricultural system, from the farmer to the government to CEOs, should be able to assess the data they need for their own utilities. That's why following the global food price hikes in 2007-08 and 2010-2012, the Agricultural Market Information System (AMIS) was launched by the G20 Ministers of Agriculture, as a measure to reduce the volatility of food markets and enhance food market transparency.[41]

In further efforts to increase market transparency, the USDA launched the Global Open Data for Agriculture and Nutrition (GODAN) initiative in 2013. With over 700 partners from the private and public sector, non-profits, and universities, GODAN promotes the proactive sharing of open data to make agriculture and nutrition information highly accessible and usable worldwide.[42] Ultimately, the initiative brings together global stakeholders to solve long-term agriculture problems, enabling fact-based, data-driven decisions all over the world.

In the next few decades, bridging the data transparency gap across global agriculture will be a key milestone. The conglomeration of big data will involve making these comprehensive and centralized data platforms highly accessible to the masses to democratize data. The institution that manages to curate all big data and government data into a single, centralized platform will be the winner.

As the 2010-2011 food price spike showed us, greater accessibility to smart and accurate data is desperately needed. The fact of the matter is that the global agriculture market is incredibly complex. Agriculture data is traditionally messy, highly vulnerable to fluctuation, and requires considerable amounts of time to sort and analyze. However, unlike in 2010, we now have sophisticated analytics tools and centralized data platforms that provide us with more dynamic and comprehensive information about our complex agricultural markets. As these capabilities become more accessible to all stakeholders, smart data will eventually lead the way to a more transparent, collaborative, and democratic agricultural system.

THE AGE OF SMART AGRICULTURE

The digitization of information and content has already profoundly disrupted traditional businesses like book publishing, the music industry, and more recently, the cable television industry. Think how Amazon digitized book sales. How Spotify and Apple music brought music online and replaced records. How Netflix and Hulu disrupted cable television.

Just like the digital information age, we're entering a smart agricultural age, where any farmer can use digital information about his/her farms to make data-driven decisions anytime, anywhere. With the commoditization of low-cost sensors and rapid developments in IoT infrastructure, the existence of smart farms will no longer be a novelty in the future. In 30 years, a majority of farms around the world should be able to have easy access to digital farm data with the touch of a device, allowing them to discover valuable insights to manage their farms better.

Additionally, the utilization of this big data in predictive analytics and forecast modeling will pave the way for a smarter agricultural system. The earth's climate is changing at an alarmingly rapid rate; we can't keep up with it and so we can't afford to be surprised. We need to arm ourselves with evidence-based forecasts and predictive analytics to be proactive in mitigating the unpredictable effects of climate change and food production instability.

The centralization of smart data in agriculture will also be a powerful advancement that provides fair economic opportunities for farmers and other agricultural stakeholders. Open access to big data and government data will be vital for agricultural market transparency. Every day, farmers, traders, and consumers around the world make decisions related to agriculture and nutrition—these decisions are only as good as the data that supports them.

By 2050, we'll move toward an era where all stakeholders, from commodity traders to smallholder farmers, will have access to smart data to reduce uncertainty and increase efficiency. We'll live in a smart data world where almost every farm will be digitized and armed with precision agriculture tools that spearhead the most productive and efficient farming practices we've ever seen.

CHAPTER 2

AGRICULTURAL ROBOTS: THE DIGITAL FARM WORKER

————

In the coming decades, the growing scarcity of farm workers will yell instability for agriculture. The farm needs a new type of farm worker. Here come the agricultural robots.

On his 450-acre farm in England's Hampshire countryside, farmer Jamie Butler has just hired a new farm worker.[1] Butler's new worker, Tom, periodically monitors his winter wheat crops for weeds and pests that are detrimental to his crop. Tom is a farmer's dream worker. He works day and night without getting tired or even breaking a sweat (and without overtime pay). He identifies weeds and pests in a field earlier and more accurately than any farm worker Butler has ever employed.

Tom is really unlike any farm worker you've seen before. He's a robot.

Created by UK-based Small Robot Company (SRC), Tom is a miniature crop and soil monitoring robot that uses GPS, artificial intelligence, and imaging technology to digitally map the field.[2] Equipped with sensors, Tom collects information about a farmer's crops and feeds that information into a neural network. Once that neural network has been fed enough information and is well-trained, SRC's machine learning software then advises Tom's two other robot co-workers, Dick and Harry, when to plant, when to feed, and when to weed the field.[3]

Workers like Tom, Dick, and Harry are becoming incredibly valuable to farmers like Jamie Butler, who reap the benefits of autonomous tools that embrace precision agriculture. At a time when the labor supply in agriculture is facing a massive shortage and issues such as the overuse of agrochemicals threatens farming, robotic workers offer a compelling alternative to human workers.

Welcome to the robotic revolution, where robots fill the agricultural labor gap and make agriculture more precise and efficient than ever.

THE AGRICULTURAL LABOR SHORTAGE

Agriculture is in a major labor shortage crisis. There are two farming jobs available for every applicant in the U.S.[4] In 2017, less than 2% of the U.S. population was involved in agriculture.[5] That percentage is only declining.

Blame it on slumping commodity prices or point fingers at unstable political climates—a big reason is that farm income is the lowest it's been in many years. In the U.S., total net farm income was projected to drop to a 12-year low of US$59.5 billion in 2018.[6] That's a more than 50% decline since the high-income levels experienced in 2013.[7]

What's even more atrocious, is that since 1996, more than 50% of U.S. farm households actually *lost* money from farming. According to the U.S. Economic Research Service, median annual on-farm household income averaged -US$1,569 between 2008 and 2014, and was projected at -US$1,316 per household in 2018 (a 15% decrease since 2017).[8] Realistically, over half of all U.S. farms are what the USDA calls residence farms—those where the primary occupation of the farm's operator is something other than farming.[9] Without off-farm income, farmers actually lose money from farming—an occupation essential to nourishing the world. Regardless, this is wildly shocking. Who works a job or runs a business that makes you lose money? Farmers, apparently.

Over in the U.K., there was a 29% shortfall in agricultural labor from 2016-2017.[10] Partly due to Brexit greatly reducing foreign farm labor, some 60% of farmers reported labor shortages in 2017.[11] Tragically, almost one in three growers had to leave their crops unharvested because they couldn't find anyone to pick them in 2017.[12] The U.K. literally had fields of ripe strawberries with no one to pluck them. That's really sad.

"Whether it's berries or lettuce or grapes, we're all scrambling for labor availability," said Scott Komar, senior vice president of R&D at U.S. berry producer Driscoll's.[13]

The labor shortage in agriculture is real. The reality is that farming is a tough and oftentimes isolating job, which easily explains the lack of interest amongst people in today's generation to begin a career in farming. In many of the interviews I have done with farmers and entrepreneurs, labor—the astounding lack of it—has been brought up countless times. Most conversations end up being about the lack of good labor, or how the majority demographic of farmers are people from older generations.

How many times have you heard someone under the age of 40 say they were or wanted to be a farmer? Pretty much none, right? Farming isn't a sexy job. It's a grueling, labor-intensive job that doesn't get enough credit in society. My guess is you'd be much more excited to get into farming if it didn't require physical labor like plowing and instead involved more high-tech methods like AI-operated growing systems or robots on fields. Maybe it's time to consider a career in high-tech farming.

The current lack of a substantial agricultural workforce yells instability for labor supply in agriculture. The lack of labor is perhaps one of the most pressing issues curtailing the agriculture industry. Clearly, a new type of non-human worker is desperately needed.

A REVOLUTION IN FARM MACHINERY

In September 2018, I was attending Upstate Capital's Future of Food conference at a dairy and vegetable farm near Syracuse, New York. As soon as I set foot on the farm, a swarm of John Deere tractors greeted me. Tractors and machinery of all shapes and sizes scattered around the field.

Tractors are the lifeblood of a farm. Recall that back in the 1940s, tractors and farming machinery started replacing horses on the farm, becoming a farmer's most essential tools to plow, seed, fertilize, and harvest. Today, the tractor is as ubiquitous on a farm as lifting equipment is in a factory. However, the problem with plowing tractors is that they are incredibly heavy machines that crush roots and compact soil. All this compaction causes poor soil health and inhibits root growth, with tractors often destroying several rows of crops at once. The inefficiencies of tractors are further exacerbated by the fact that they limit the working window of farmers (you can't use heavy tractors when the field is too wet).

Moreover, tractors are highly inaccurate vehicles to manage crops; they spray fertilizers and chemicals across large swaths of land, often resulting in the overuse of chemicals and nutrient runoff in groundwater systems and fields. Just like patients in a hospital, individual crops have unique needs and require different levels of treatment. You wouldn't prescribe an antibiotic for everyone in a hospital—not every patient needs it. Similarly, crops in a field need different levels of treatment in order to thrive. The fault with the tractor is that it only allows the farmer to manage the farm at the field level, not the individual plant level.

While tractors have automated farm jobs like plowing, they are neither efficient nor environmentally friendly—plowing tractors use 95% of the energy used on a farm.[14] We need an alternative to heavy, inaccurate tractors. That's where robots like Small Robot Company's come in.

Recall SRC's robots Tom, Dick, and Harry from the beginning of this chapter. The combination of imaging technology and AI-driven precision agriculture means that SRC's robots feed, weed, and spray only the plants that need it, providing the perfect amounts of nutrients and pesticides needed by each plant to thrive. The use of these robots actually allow farmers to use 90% less chemicals and 95% less energy, significantly reducing costs.[15] On top of that, the lightness of SRC's agile and light robots reduces heavy compaction of soil—the issue that tractors fail to avoid. Unlike human-driven tractors, robots can also operate 24/7, increasing the working window available to farmers.[16]

When I first spoke to Ben Scott-Robinson and Sam Watson Jones, co-founders of the SRC, it was clear that they were on a mission to make digital farming exist in a sustainable and efficient way in the future. Sam, a fourth-generation farmer, knew that his tractors were only designed to be powerful and to get across the field as fast as possible. It wasn't designed to be as accurate and precise as a farmer like him needed it to be. Upon recognizing that farmers need unique and personalized solutions, Sam and Ben got together to build SRC. Today, SRC's lightweight, agile robots are enabling farmers to get accurate data about their fields.[17]

Perhaps the most fundamental change that is occurring as agricultural small robots become our farm workers, is this shift in farm management decisions from the field level to the plant level. Currently, most farms manage their farms by the field level, meaning all plants are treated as if they have the same needs. In reality, that isn't the case. Each individual plant has unique needs, just as each patient at a hospital has different needs.

The combination of robotics and machine learning capabilities in agriculture is allowing farmers to know which specific plants require more inputs. With this level of intelligence, farmers can optimize input use and reduce nutrient runoff in order to enhance productivity and profitability. This is only possible by changing outdated and inefficient machinery like tractors that have existed for decades.

Agricultural robots like SRC's are disrupting the ownership of existing machinery like tractors, which have traditionally failed to serve the needs of the farmer. Overtime, small robots will help reduce farming's negative impacts on the environment and increase farm productivity by extending the working time available to the farmer. Soon, the rapid development of smart agriculture robots and powerful AI systems will eventually allow farmers to replace tractors altogether.

THE WEED CONTROL CRISIS

In October 2014, Blue River Technologies, an agricultural robot company, launched its first product—the Lettuce-Bot.[18] Used on fields with young lettuce plants, the Lettuce-Bot has embedded cameras that use computer vision and machine learning software to distinguish between crops and weeds, with automated sprayers that direct chemicals only on unwanted plants.[19]

Three years later in September 2017, John Deere acquired Blue River Technologies for a whopping US$305 million (Blue River Technologies only raised a little over US$30 million in capital before being acquired).[20] By then, LettuceBot was already being used in over 10% of U.S. lettuce production.[21]

Today, its "See and Spray" weed control robot can reportedly reduce agrochemical use (and therefore costs) by 90%. Using computer vision and AI, Blue River Technologies' smart machines can detect, identify, and make management decisions about every single plant in the field.[22]

Kiersten Stead, managing partner of Data Collective Venture Capital and previous investment director at Monsanto Growth Ventures (MGV), says after the acquisition:

"Today, Blue River Technology's robotic implements are weeding in cotton fields using contact herbicides with high

accuracy, and over a 90% reduction in chemistry applications. "See and spray" will clearly be another tool for farmers who need to cope with weed suppression of yield and herbicide resistance.

We can now see a legitimate path to a utopian time-not-too-far-away, where "see and spray"... can be used to tend each plant individually. This is the start of the next chapter in agriculture." [23]

Smart, autonomous machines like SRC's and Blue River Technologies' are revolutionizing weed control in an agricultural world of mass herbicide resistance. The overuse and over-reliance of harmful agrochemicals with non-targeted spraying has meant that over 250 species of weeds worldwide are now resistant to weed control chemicals. That's not great news. It means that despite the need to produce more food in the coming decades, we'll have trouble doing so due to highly resilient weeds.

Simply put, the health and productivity of farms relies on the elimination of pests and weeds that interfere with successful crop production. Solutions like Blue River Technologies' See & Spray robots will play a key role in a future where smart, autonomous machines give farmers a new way to control and prevent herbicide-resistant weeds, while also eliminating the mass overuse of agrochemicals.

The acquisition of Blue River Technologies by a farm machinery company like John Deere is significant and revealing. It signals the optimism that traditional farm machinery players have for machine-learning based, autonomous robots.

It signals that robots will play a key role in the future of precision agriculture and weed control. Most of all, it signals the fear that these traditional farm machinery companies have of being replaced.

AUTOMATION, NOT JUST AUGMENTATION

The arrival of robots means it is no longer about augmentation on the farm, it is really about automation. Not only do agricultural robots help farmers make plant-level decisions, they autonomously act on those decisions, just as the SRC robots Dick and Harry seed, feed, and weed for the farmer.

Even the act of picking delicate fruits like tomatoes and strawberries has become increasingly automated. Robotic picker startup Soft Robotics has successfully developed a robotic gripping system that can effectively pick fragile produce as well as—but faster—than the human hand.[24] Of course, this predominantly works best in conventional fields with standard crop heights. Employing robotic pickers on a small field in India growing 15 different crop varieties on small plots of land would be significantly less feasible. These are challenges that will be overcome as sensing and imaging capabilities in robots become increasingly sophisticated.

In the future, the farm could be completely autonomous, while also being profitable. At UC Davis, researchers have developed a "no touch" vineyard, where autonomous machines do everything. A robotic irrigation system directed by sensors waters the vines. Robotic pickers harvest the grapes. The system is incredibly efficient in yield, quality, and cost; it allows for around 40 more plants per acre and costs around 7 cents per vine in labor, compared to US$1 per vine in a conventional vineyard.[25] Frankly, that's incredible.

The future of agricultural robots looks bright. The agricultural robot market is expected to grow from US$2.8 billion in 2016 to US$12.8 billion by 2022, at a CAGR (compounded annual growth rate) of 20.71% between 2017 and 2022.[26] Considering the widening farm labor gap and the need for more precise agriculture, the market for agricultural robots is accelerating.

Phil Erlanger, managing director and co-founder of Agri-Tech focused VC firm Pontifax AgTech, speaks to the mass opportunities offered by robotics in agriculture:

"Robotics stands to solve some key issues in agriculture including sustainability concerns, such as reducing chemical loads, labor shortages, and the use of data to allow for more precise and efficient production of crops."[27]

Gene Munster, managing partner of Loup Ventures is also optimistic about the future of agricultural robots: "I think agriculture is the greatest near-term—I define over the next five years—opportunity around robotics and autonomy."[28] The lack of significant barriers to entry like red tape on open fields is a huge advantage that agricultural robots have over other autonomous systems like drones (which face a lot of airspace regulation). This, plus the agricultural labor shortage, helps create "a wonderful intersection between robotics and agriculture," according to Munster.[29]

Integrated computer vision technology and artificial intelligence capabilities are ensuring that smart, autonomous machines can do the things that humans currently aren't able to do (at least effectively) in agriculture. Things like detecting which individual plants require variable amounts of herbicide. Things like delicately picking soft fruit fast. Things like not heavily compacting soil while working it with a tractor or by foot.

In the future, agricultural robots like milking robots and robotic pickers will play an immense role in field crop and animal management. Robots like SRC's and Blue River Technologies' offer precision agriculture solutions that give farmers the level of data granularity needed to improve crop yields with minimal resource and labor use.

In Chapter 1, I discussed the power of smart data in arming farmers with the tools needed to make better agronomic decisions. The farmer might be smart, but they still have to act on that data. What do we do when we don't have enough farmers to act on this data? What do we do when there is a lack of farmers to even drive a tractor or carry out jobs like seeding? What do we do when humans are incapable of spraying precise amounts of agrochemicals on specific crops that need it? We look to robots.

WILL ROBOTS STEAL OUR JOBS?

The common gut reaction to the idea of robots entering our workforce is that they will steal our jobs. While they do replace tasks like weeding and seeding, they will ultimately change and enhance the farmer's job. Just as automation transformed manufacturing, the farmer's job will eventually evolve. Ben, co-founder of the SRC, told me something that profoundly changed my entire view of automation. He said that robots "free up humanity to move away from being slaves to menial jobs."[30] There's a huge case to adopt robots on the field.

By putting this mundane labor burden on robots, farmers will only need to spend 20% of their time on things that generate 80% of their income.[31] This means farmers will now have more time to pursue other avenues of generating value and making money. For instance, they could dedicate this freed-up time to agri-tourism (an industry worth more than food production in the UK) or creating high-value specialty food products.[32] As farms become increasingly autonomous, the farmer's job will become more diversified, which will have a profound impact on rural economic development. The time freed up from autonomous systems will help create new businesses and encourage the development of new skills in rural communities. Ultimately, a farmer will no longer just maintain farms and sell crops in the future.

As I think about the automation of our farms, I'd equate the robotic revolution to the industrial revolution, where repetitive manufacturing jobs in the factory were replaced by machinery and new production systems for the better. For example, warehouse logistics and mining are examples of industries that have hugely benefited from autonomous systems replacing menial, repetitive, and grueling jobs.

Amazon's warehouses are operated mainly by robots, which make distribution incredibly effective and enable the consumer to enjoy highly convenient deliveries and affordable products. The emergence of 'Smart Mines', which incorporates everything from robotic drills to self-driving ore trucks, has made the miner's job significantly safer compared to pure manual labor.[33]

While many would argue that the mechanization and automation of these jobs have robbed thousands of a source of income, menial jobs like selecting and lifting inventory or mining are considered dangerous and highly repetitive ones. If Amazon hadn't come around to automate warehouse logistics, much of the world would still be stuck in highly inefficient ways of managing inventory and delivering goods. Instead, automation allowed the workforce to eliminate inefficiency, adapt, and develop skills in other pertinent areas like artificial intelligence. Automation essentially evolved the job of someone working in logistics. In the process, it also allowed new business models like Amazon Prime and 2-day shipping to unlock new value for consumers.

Similarly, there is a case for using robots to automate menial farm tasks. Tasks like plowing are inherently low-wage; they are menial jobs that usually can't be paid more than the minimum wage, or else food prices would be far too high. As with all industries, disruptions must occur to make way for new value and opportunities to be unlocked.

Furthermore, replacing physical human labor in agriculture and therefore moving people out of agriculture can also be beneficial for global economic development. Dr. Prabhu Pingali, founding director of the Tata-Cornell Institute and professor in the Charles H. Dyson School of Applied Economics and Management and Division of Nutritional Sciences at Cornell University, argues that transitioning people, especially in rural areas, out of agriculture is a key aspect of economic development in developing countries:[34]

"If you look historically, you'll see the share of population in agriculture drops with economic growth. It's happened around the world. It's happened in Malaysia, it's happening in India, it's happening in Thailand. The share of population living in rural areas and depending on agriculture simply drops as economic development takes place. That is a fact of life... we've seen this historically and there's no reason why that won't continue to be the case."[35]

As economic development and urbanization takes place in developing nations, being a farmer becomes less appealing and less lucrative as a job. Yet, the world still needs to produce enough food to sustain its population. With the downturn of agricultural labor supply, the continuation and success of agriculture requires automation more than ever.

While the advent of robots will make some of today's farm jobs obsolete, history has shown us that if there is a will, there is a way. Robots are just another step in a long history of mechanization and automation serving society. They will simply free up time spent on labor-intensive, repetitive tasks so that farmers in developing countries can pursue other opportunities that create high value and generate more income.

THE FUTURE OF THE DIGITAL FARM WORKER

A robotic agriculture evolution is underway. The integration of computer vision, robotics, and machine learning will increasingly enable us to use smart, autonomous machines to collect data, derive actionable insights, and act on field management decisions at the plant level.

Ultimately, there is a fundamental need to fill the labor gap in agriculture. Japan's imminent scarcity of caretakers to care for their aging population prompted them to become leaders in robot caretakers. In the same way, the next few decades will see agriculture suffering from a lack of farm workers; robots will act as those farm workers. However, fear not, robots won't completely replace farmers. They will merely evolve the farmer's job and bring about a myriad of new opportunities.

The automation of labor-intensive, menial farming jobs is here to stay. By 2050, agricultural robots will create semi-autonomous, smart farms that are highly efficient, green, and most of all, profitable. By 2050, agriculture robots will make farmers' jobs more interesting, allowing them to swap mundane jobs like weeding for high-income jobs in agri-tourism or specialty foods, all while maintaining the same agricultural outputs.

In the future, farms like the dairy and vegetable farm I visited in Syracuse, New York can replace the role of a tractor with a far more efficient and precise way of managing the farm. Instead of a landscape dotted with human field workers and John Deere tractors, the future landscape of farms will look more like an army of robot field workers.

CHAPTER 3

DRONES: A FARMER'S EYES IN THE SKY

———

What if farmers could see everything about their fields from the sky, instead of just the ground? What if a smart flying machine could go where no tractor could? What if these machines could pollinate crops in a world without honeybees? Enter drones—a farmer's eyes in the sky.

Meet Scout, one of the world's fully autonomous drones for farmers. Scout lives in a box that resembles a large beehive and takes off several times a day to collect multi-spectral images of nearby farm fields.[1] When not in use, Scout returns to its box, recharges its batteries, downloads captured images, stitches maps together, and uploads the processed data to a cloud-based system, which the farmer can access from any device, anytime, anywhere.[2]

Wake up, launch, fly a mission, go home, process images, recharge batteries, send data and stitched images to the cloud. Scout does this more than four or five times a day—all without the need for a pilot or operator. Someone in a remote location could literally program Scout to perform these tasks for up to a year at a time.

Drones like Scout are part of the future landscape of agriculture.

The power of the drone lies in its ability to quickly collect vast, spatial data with great accuracy and speed. The same devices use machine learning algorithms to analyze images and data into actionable information. They also have the ability to carry out a range of tasks like crop spraying and pollinating.

Drone planters that shoot pods with seeds and add nutrients to the soil. Aerial spraying drones that spray precise amounts of pesticides and fertilizers with even coverage. Aerial imaging that monitors crop conditions and detects diseases early. Drone sensors that detect dry areas to maintain water irrigation.

In the future of agricultural drones, would a farmer even need to work on a farm day to day?

THE POWER OF AUTONOMOUS
EYES IN THE SKY

Since the 1920s, manned aircraft has been used to collect information about farmland resources and in early detection systems to manage locust outbreaks.[3] The trouble with aircraft? They are expensive to fly, require a licensed pilot, and have local hindrances.

Another form of aerial monitoring involves using satellite imagery to assess crop distribution and health. The drawback of satellite imaging? Satellite images have to be ordered in advance, can only be taken once a day, are extremely costly, and are imprecise and lacking in detail.[4]

Currently, aerial imaging companies use manned aircraft to fly across fields and collect data. However, due to aircraft and satellite imaging's lack of precision, farms still have to hire crop scouts, farm workers that go out and physically inspect fields, to identify specific parts of the field that need a farmer's attention. Moreover, the only way to prematurely detect diseases in crops is for crop scouts to collect plant samples and send them to a DNA lab for processing. Basically, current methods of crop assessment and disease detection take large amounts of time and manpower and aren't always accurate.

That's where drones like Scout win for the farmer.

Drones, also known as UAVs (unmanned aerial vehicles), offer significant benefits over these traditional remote sensing methods. Firstly, UAVs are autonomous; no need for human crop scouts or samples to be sent to a lab. Furthermore, drones fly at low altitudes and speeds, making them capable of capturing extremely high-resolution images and data.

Compared to current satellite imaging methods, drone-derived data is much more comprehensive and detailed. Once a drone like Scout has completed a flight, the captured images and data is processed using various analytic tools; the resulting information provides incredibly precise, accurate, and actionable insights for farmers to manage crops at the plant level.[5] Essentially, drones allow farmers to efficiently obtain a birds-eye-view of their crops, detecting subtle changes that cannot be readily identified by satellites or crop scouts at the ground level.

In Malaysia and Indonesia, palm oil company IOI Group has used drones to digitally map its palm oil plantations and provide data on estate plant density in order to discern the appropriate planting distance between seeds.[6] In the palm oil business, determining the appropriate planting distance between seeds is highly significant. Why? Let's just say, palm trees aren't particularly polite trees. From the trees' upper crown, a wild jungle of sprawling, sharp leaves called fronds fan out along protruding branches. Fronds grow to be 30-45 feet (9-14m) long and 4 -8 feet (1-2m) wide.[7]

Considering this, it's crucial that enough space exists between trees, so that trees can grow to its full size without having to fight for space with other trees. At the same time, plant seeds too far apart and the productivity of the entire estate dramatically goes down with lower yields per hectare. For a company like IOI that maintains 90 oil palm estates covering a total of 217,329 hectares (537,032 acres),[8] using drones to analyze its estates has become indispensable in providing previously unattainable information when making decisions like planting distance.

As data-processing applications and analytics tools become less expensive and easier to use in the future, the cost reductions resulting from using agricultural drones will be highly significant, especially with a labor shortage in agriculture. The market for agricultural drones is estimated to be worth US$32.4 billion, second only to infrastructure amongst the value of drone solutions in all applicable industries.[9] Even Goldman Sachs has predicted that the agriculture sector will be the second largest user of drones in the world by 2021.[10]

Joel Wipperfurth, Director of Agriculture Technology for WinField United, believes farmers desperately need the level of autonomy and insights offered by agricultural drones: "Farmers want to capitalize on opportunities to boost both crop health and yield potential throughout the season, but they can't walk every acre, every day. We believe autonomy will be a key component to the success of in-season scouting technology."[11]

Clearly, farmers want to embrace the benefits of using agricultural drones. Between 2017-2018, the use of drones in agriculture has flourished; according to an April 2018

Munich Reinsurance America survey of 269 U.S. farmers, three in four U.S. farmers (74%) are currently using or considering adopting the technology to assess, monitor, and manage their farm.[12]

Moreover, adoption is skyrocketing with a mind-boggling number of drones now flying. The yearly sales of small UAVs reached 400,000 units in the Federal Republic of Germany in 2016 and in the U.S., sales of drones more than doubled in the year ending February 2017, with a year-over-year increase of 117%.[13]

Jason Dunn, Strategic Products Expert at Munich Reinsurance America, Inc. summarizes the major wins of agricultural drones: "Whether a farm has less than 100 or more than 5,000 acres, drones can be the eyes and ears for farmers that want to efficiently and cost effectively monitor and manage crops, livestock, and soil conditions."[14]

The use of UAVs in agriculture is ushering in a new agricultural revolution by replacing the use of traditionally time-consuming, inaccurate, and climate sensitive satellite imaging.

PREDICTIVE CROP MAINTENANCE

Being a farmer is extremely hard as it is. Erratic weather conditions, dwindling crop prices, the rising costs of pollination, and the infestation of pests and diseases are just some of the big issues farmers face.

One of the fairly unavoidable challenges for farmers is dealing with the unwelcome arrival of pests and diseases. In developing countries, 40-50% of all crop yields are lost due to pests, diseases, or post-harvest losses.[15] That's a significant loss of efficiency and yield—40 to 50% less than we can afford in a resource-scarce future.

Currently, the approach farmers have towards pests and disease is a very reactionary one, not a preventative one. The fundamental norm is that farmers spray crops to get rid of pests and potential diseases. That's what the entire US$215 billion agrochemical industry is built on.[16] But often, it's too late once a disease or pest arrives. The reality is that many disease or pest-infested crops are incredibly hard to salvage and stop from spreading.

Take citrus greening—an invasive disease common in the citrus industry—as an example. The disease is incredibly hard to spot with the naked eye and is often only detected after an infestation has occurred. Once detected, it is too late to salvage a field of crops, especially since there is no cure once a tree is infected.[17] It's safe to say that air-borne pathogens and invasive diseases like citrus greening can be extremely detrimental to global crop production.

Interestingly, researchers at Virginia Tech have successfully used drones to detect high-flying, airborne plant pathogens before they even land on fields of crops.[18] Using drones to sample plant pathogens in the lower atmosphere is incredibly beneficial; if a farmer knows of a disease or pathogen outbreak in a nearby area, they could be alerted early of its eventual arrival and put in place preventative measures to ensure it doesn't spread. If states could monitor air-borne pathogens on a large scale, they could essentially alert farmers and equip them with the tools to mitigate an outbreak.[19]

With the development of advanced spectral sensing technology, drones are able to measure particular wavelengths of light absorbed and reflected by plants, which help generate images that highlight problem areas in a field down to the plant level. Since stressed or dehydrated crops reflect light differently, this method of spectral imaging allows the farmer to accurately spot weak crops and parts of the field prematurely.

The use of drones in early disease detection and crop assessments is essentially what predictive maintenance in the industrial Internet of Things is to agriculture. In industrial fields like manufacturing, predictive maintenance is the practice of using data collected from machines and equipment in order to predict and prevent a deficiency or breakdown before it occurs. In the same way, spectral imaging using drones is providing the farmer with the data insights required to prevent their crops from pest and pathogen infestation before it is too late. While such predictive insights are a norm in other industries, detecting the spread of diseases and pests at this level of accuracy, efficiency, and predictability has never been seen before in agriculture.

In the future, drones will provide immense opportunities to create better crop monitoring and disease detection systems. With its power to collect data from an aerial view, drones will increasingly act as a farm's smart inspector, detecting weak plants that might need additional treatment and unwanted pests and diseases before it's too late. In the future, we'll be saying hello to Scout the Drone and bidding human crop scouts goodbye.

THE ALTERNATIVE POLLINATOR

In early 2015, New York-based startup Dropcopter completed the first ever automated drone pollination of orchard crops in the U.S. In its initial trials, it managed to boost the crop set of almond orchards by at least 10%.[20] Its patent-pending UAV is able to fly on an autonomous route and distribute precisely measured amounts of pollen directly over crops—I call it precision pollination.

Since its first trial in 2015, it has had significant success; from 2015-2018, it was able to use drone pollinators to pollinate almond, cherry, and apple orchards and achieve dramatic crop set increases of 25%-60%.[21] The future of pollination could very much lie in aerial drone pollinators like Dropcopter's.

It isn't old news that bees are dying; there has been a 40% loss of commercial honeybees in the U.S. from 2006 to 2013.[22] In the UK, there has been a 45% loss between 2010 and 2013.[23] This is devastating for the state of agriculture. Why? Because bees are key enablers in our food system—a third of the food we eat is directly dependent on pollinating bees.[24] Between US$235 billion and US$577 billion worth of annual food production relies on direct contributions by pollinators.[25] In fact, 84% of all commercially grown crops are insect pollinated.[26] So yes, bees and other pollinators are extremely important for our food systems. A world without pollinators would be unimaginably disastrous for feeding the world.

The decline of bees is having a debilitating impact on farmers; since 2008, the price of bee pollination has increased by 100%.[27] The heavy costs of bee pollination cuts into farmers margins and raises the price of food at the grocery store. Without an alternative pollination method, we could soon see the price of our apples, peaches, and almonds skyrocket to unprecedented levels. Imagine how much more expensive your almond milk would be.

Adam Fine, the co-founder and CTO of Dropcopter, tells me about the urgent pollination problem Dropcopter is tackling:

"I'm pretty certain that the decline of bee pollinators is a global problem. Over the past 25 years, the world has lost one-third of its insect biomass, which is a scary figure since 80% of all species on Earth are insects. At the same time, rising populations and changing climates mean we're going to have less arable land and fresh water to feed the 9 billion or more people that will be on this planet in the next 50 years."[28]

Adam speaks passionately about the pressing problem of bee pollination decline. Interestingly enough, the idea for

Dropcopter started as "an ill-fated idea to deliver food on golf courses using drone aircraft."[29] Adam then met Matt Koball, a farmer and eventual co-founder and CEO of Dropcopter. Speaking to farmers at Matt's orchard in California, Adam clearly noticed that a major problem faced was the unreliability of bee pollination. Adam discovered that for farmers, it was a constant struggle to get crops pollinated properly. Without knowing when and if bees would come, farmers relied solely on their crop insurance.

Solutions like Dropcopter's give me hope that drones could one day replace bees. Think about it—bees fly from plant to plant carrying and depositing nectar and pollen as it lands on each flower. With the advancement of drones, we could technically use drones to do the same thing—fly from plant to plant to deposit pollen and nectar.

Aerial drone pollination solves another problem farmers face—bees can't fly at night due to cold temperatures, but drones can. This means aerial drone pollinators can double the pollination windows for farmers by also flying at night, when flowers are open. This has a huge impact on farmers, who are often at the mercy of adverse temperatures and bee scarcity affecting their crops. With drone pollinators, farmers can pollinate their crops when bees are unavailable or when bad weather prevents bees from flying.

With US$235 billion-US$577 billion worth of global food production at stake, aerial drone pollination will play an important role in the future of our global food system.[30]

It offers farmers a fast, reliable, and effective pollination method that alleviates the increasing costs of bee pollination and delivers a profit for farmers through minimal resource use and efficiency gains.

When pollinating bees decline to the point of extinction, who is going to pollinate the crops that make up a third of the food we eat? Drones.

REGULATION, DATA PRIVACY, AND SAFETY

Despite adding tremendous value on the farm, the commercialization of agricultural drones will face several challenges. Namely, regulatory barriers limiting flight operations, privacy infringement concerns associated with spatial data, and the safety of UAV use in farming.

One of the biggest challenges is in regulation. A key thing to note here is actually the *lack* of global regulation standards. Currently, regulations vary significantly across countries and globally recognized Remote Pilot Certificate (RPC) standards have not been developed.

For instance, the U.S. Federal Aviation Administration (FAA) has stated a strict "no flying over people" rule, with a restriction of at least 25ft. (8m) away from people and property.[31] In contrast, the Australian Civil Aviation Safety Authority (CASA) permits drone operation within 49-98 ft. (15-30m) of a person.[32] In the U.K., the Civil Aviation Authority (CAA) states that drones must stay at least 150ft. (50m) away from people and property.[33]

It's safe to say that it is a struggle to discern a standard set of rules that apply to all drone operations, which will prove to be challenging for drone companies hoping to scale globally. With differing regulation, drone operators must be very diligent in adhering to rules stipulated in each country; another layer of legal red tape that may deter commercial drone innovation.

However, there are common operational practices that are pretty standard across the industry. Flying within a visual line of sight (VLOS) is one of them. Generally, this refers to a minimum distance between the aerial vehicle and the remote pilot so that the pilot can see the drone.[34] In Europe, Australia, and the U.S., the maximum VLOS is set at no more than 400ft. (120m) vertically above ground level and a 1640 ft. (500m) horizontal radius around the remote pilot.[35]

However, these VLOS restrictions are crippling for fully autonomous drones that want to fly missions without a pilot. That's when Beyond Visual Line of Site (BVLOS) operations emerged. Unlike VLOS, BVLOS operations involve flight outside of the pilot's locale and sight.[36] Currently, this type of operation is still being appealed for, but with assistive technologies that can effectively sense and avoid objects, BVLOS operations in low-risk environments like rural farms can be conducted safely.

Think back to Scout, the autonomous drone created by American Robotics. The lack of BVLOS legality actually prevents Scout from being commercialized. However, American

Robotics' CEO, Reese Mozer, is optimistic about improving Scout's technology to be ready for BVLOS operations: "It's a bit of a misconception that we're just waiting on the FAA to just change their regulations. We know what they want us to achieve and that's safe flight and that's a technical issue. It's a central focus of this company and we're confident that we will have a solution soon."[37]

Basically, in order for drones to be 100% autonomous, BVLOS operations must be legalized. There is still a lot of work to get there, but the regulatory issue is arguably counterintuitive. As Mozer has stated, it is not strictly a regulatory issue, but also a technical one involving the demonstration of operational safety. In other words, if drone companies like American Robotics can prove that BVLOS operations is safe for all stakeholders involved, regulation will give way.

As drone regulation starts to standardize and the ambiguity associated with flying dissipates, companies—small and large—will increasingly opt to use them on the farm. But while regulation is necessary, having too stringent regulation could stifle the growth of drone innovation on the farm. Just look at the adoption of agricultural drones in China. China initially had little commercial drone regulation, which enabled it to see much faster developments in agricultural drone applications compared to the U.S., especially in pesticide spraying. Other countries like South Africa have even more restrictive regulations that ultimately pose significant challenges to a thriving agriculture drone industry.

On the flipside, a lack of regulation could also pose significant safety concerns. In 2017, 240 flights in Southwest China were disrupted by drones, leaving 10,000 travelers stranded at an airport.[38] The lack of stipulated guidelines and uncertainty in liability allowed the drones to fly into unwanted and unsafe territory. Eventually, China's municipal Public Security Bureau took measures to ramp up drone regulation, stipulating fines of up to 5,000 yuan (US$744) to anyone who violates drone regulation.[39]

Another challenge in UAV operations is in data privacy and ownership. As countries in the EU and other nations ramp up on data privacy regulation, there is no question that commercial drone operators will increasingly need to worry about privacy issues; the aforementioned survey by Munich Reinsurance America found that out of the 76% of respondents that have drone usage concerns, the highest percentage (23%) cited data privacy issues as a major concern.[40] While the data collected from drones provides immense value to farmers, it remains ambiguous who owns the data collected and who has the right to analyze, compile, and distribute it.

Keith Gingerich, the third-generation, digital-savvy farmer mentioned in Chapter 1, states his views on farm data ownership: "I believe that field data is owned by the owner/operator of the land that is writing the check for the particular operation. Whoever owns the equipment should have access to the machine part of the data and the landowner should own the application data."[41]

The conversation on data ownership and privacy gets fuzzier as we consider farmers who contract out drone imaging and services versus farmers who handle their own drone usage and analytics. Cyber security is also a major threat; farmers face the risk of third parties hacking a drone and using it for dangerous actions. Overtime, governments, drone operators, drone analytics services, and aerial imaging companies will require greater cooperation to ensure data privacy is preserved and cyber security measures are implemented.

Favorable drone regulation, clear data privacy stipulations, and better cyber security solutions will be instrumental for the widespread commercialization of agricultural drones. In particular, governments will play a key role in helping to build systems that support and facilitate the growth of innovative drone-powered solutions in agriculture.

While agricultural drones hold a bright future for farmers, its mass adoption is still fraught with challenges. But challenges can be overcome if clear added value is demonstrated. We've seen this in other industries; for instance, the concept of home-sharing initially faced safety and legal challenges. Yet, when there is an overwhelming need, challenges such as regulation make way for adoption. Today, home-sharing is a US$37 billion market in the U.S.[42]

Similarly, companies like American Robotics and Dropcopter will be able to continually improve its proposition and work with regulatory bodies to ensure that challenges are resolved for the widespread adoption of agricultural drones.

Considering the great opportunities offered by UAVs for agriculture, overly restrictive regulations over drone usage could hinder developments in this space. Of course, a balance between public safety (regulation) and accessibility to commerce is critical. I believe the industry will find that balance and come to a conclusion as to the extent of regulation and the positive externalities offered by innovative drone solutions.

GLOBAL DRONE ADOPTION

It was summer 2017 in the Heilongjiang province of Northern China. Across vast swaths of rice paddy fields and vegetable patches, it's impossible to not hear the incessant buzz of drones or catch a glimpse of these magical flying vehicles.[43]

Heilongjiang, which spans more than 13 million hectares of flat, fertile farmland, churns out more agricultural products than any other province in China.[44] To give you a sense of the scale of its production, its annual food output is enough to feed everyone in China (1.4 billion people) for nearly two months.[45]

However, like many other rural parts of the world facing increasing urbanization, Heilongjiang's agriculture sector is facing a growing labor shortage. Young people are flocking to the city in search of better paying jobs and less grueling work. Few want to work in the rice paddy fields that provide sustenance for much of the province. And as if urbanization wasn't detrimental enough for agriculture's labor supply in the area, many people choose to opt out of these jobs that involve highly toxic agrochemicals.

"Drones are saving us," said Liu Jun, a farmer from the village of Dongan in Heilongjiang who helped set up Dongan's "drone squadron."[46] More than 20 young people in the village were trained to become professional drone pilots that year. A year before, only one person did.

Liu speaks to the increasing adoption of drones in agriculture:

"That [the use of drones] wasn't the case last year. Then, boom, there were drones everywhere. And they're doing all the dirty and harmful work such as spraying crops with pesticides and disease prevention drugs. Overnight, their [farmers'] performance [in the agriculture sector] has changed farmers' suspicions of new technology. Now almost every farming family in our village has either bought or hired a drone."[47]

The financial and practical benefits of agricultural drones for farmers in these areas are clear. Employing drones reduces the labor costs for farmers, since it eliminates the need to recruit many field workers to spray pesticides. It also reduces the need for farmers to have to deal with hazardous chemicals that could be detrimental to human health. With better and more precise crop spraying capabilities than traditional aircraft and even farmers themselves, drones are becoming a ubiquitous tool in farms beyond the Heilongjiang province.

"What has happened in my village can happen in many other villages across China. Even older farmers are now embracing the technology," Liu said.[48]

"Old Chinese farmers drive tractors. Modern Chinese farmers fly drones."

And that, summarizes the future of drones in agriculture.

While China, the U.S., and Japan have been early adopters of agricultural drones, other countries have also started adopting UAVs in agriculture.

Over in the east of the Philippines, the UN Food and Agriculture Organization (FAO) has used drones equipped with special sensors to calculate indexes such as the Normalized Difference Vegetation Index (NDVI), which differentiates soil from grass or forest, detects plants under stress, and differentiates between crop stages.[49] Indexes like the NDVI provide farmers with key information affecting crop development—water stress, nutrient deficiency, pest infestation, and crop diseases. Armed with this information, farmers in the Philippines can monitor crop conditions in real time and detect diseases efficiently and prematurely.

José Luis Fernández, an FAO Representative in the Philippines, speaks to the opportunities offered by agricultural drones:

"The adoption of modern technologies in agriculture, such as the use of drones or unmanned aerial vehicles (UAVs) can significantly enhance risk and damage assessments and revolutionize the way we prepare for and respond to disasters that

affect the livelihoods of vulnerable farmers and fishers and the country's food security."[50]

Aerial monitoring efforts like the FAO's deployments in East Philippines will become increasingly mainstream as awareness of the value of drones spreads. Once analyzed, the data acquired from drones provide incredibly valuable insights that allow farmers to mitigate risk and the government to plan for disaster relief and response. The FAO's efforts proved so effective that drones have already been included in the FAO's disaster risk reduction and management (DRRM) and climate change adaptation (CCA) strategies.

Over the next few decades, countries like India, Vietnam, and Thailand, which depend heavily on agriculture, will face increasing urbanization and a declining agricultural workforce. Currently, adoption is relatively low in these areas since the capabilities to analyze and collect data from drones is limited. However, as the cost of data storage decreases and the accessibility of data analytics and imaging capabilities improves, the use of drones will soon play a major role in filling the void of grueling and harmful farming jobs in these agriculture-rich countries.

As explored in Chapter 2, "Agricultural Robots: The Digital Farm Worker," the role that autonomous tools will play in filling the agricultural labor gap is highly significant for the future of food production. Despite the aforementioned barriers like upfront capital costs and the lack of technology infrastructure in developing countries, the rural province of Heilongjiang and the FAO's efforts in East Philippines have shown that where agriculture is prevalent and an agricultural labor shortage exists, adoption of autonomous systems can and will occur.

THE FUTURE OF A FARMER'S EYES IN THE SKY

The adoption of drones in agriculture will completely revolutionize the way we assess crops and detect diseases and pests across fields. Furthermore, drone pollinators could ultimately save us from the negative impacts of the great bee decline. After all, honey bees are arguably the single most important enabler of our food production systems.

Ultimately, the use of drones to collect high-resolution spatial data will shift farming from being reactive to being more proactive. Just like predictive maintenance in manufacturing ensures a future breakdown is detected prematurely, drones ensure farmers can better predict and prepare for potential dangers that ultimately affect their livelihoods.

Although commercial deployment of autonomous drones in agriculture are still limited by technical, legal, and safety concerns, many companies like Amazon, Wal-Mart, DHL, and UPS are actively experimenting with them; ultimately, this signals a place for drone operations in agriculture. Like most disruptions, it takes time and patience for regulatory pathways to become smoother. Soon, the many exciting opportunities offered by drones will materialize in the industry, driving key solutions to major global food issues like the decline of pollinating bees.

Along with the agricultural IoT, AI, and robots, drones will be critical in the next agricultural revolution driven by smart data. By combining a whole host of data, images, and analytics, farmers will be able to build the most optimal and productive food systems. The myriad applications of a set of "eyes in the sky" are limited only by our imagination. Without a doubt, the use of drones to automate and optimize farm management and to pollinate our crops will play a key role in tackling our future's most pressing food production problems.

PART II

NOVEL FARMING
SYSTEMS

CHAPTER 4

INDOOR FARMS: THE ADVENT OF URBAN AGRICULTURE

———

Today, agriculture is no longer limited by geography and climate. The image of the rural farm is slowly dissipating. Welcome to a world where the farm and the city are one.

Emirates Airlines is one of the world's largest airlines, serving and feeding thousands of passengers on board almost 500 flights daily.[1] Unsurprisingly, it operates one of the largest food production facilities in the world. At the Emirates Flight Catering Facility (EKFC), 180,000 meals are prepared daily.[2] That's about 55 million meals a year. Each year, the facility goes through 27 tonnes of fresh broccoli, 1,210 tonnes of tomatoes, and 334 tonnes of lettuce.[3]

All this produce usually comes from traditional outdoor farms in the United Arab Emirates. By 2020, all this produce will come from an indoor vertical farm instead.

The indoor farm, a joint venture between EKFC and U.S.-based Crop One Holdings, is able to produce 6,000 pounds (2,722 kg) of high-quality, chemical-free vegetables daily, using 99% less water compared to outdoor fields.[4] To be located near Dubai International Airport, the proximity of the farm to EKFC's production facility substantially reduces carbon emissions associated with food miles. Quicker delivery also means fresher and more nutrient-retaining products that reach consumers within mere hours of harvest.

While only 130,000 square feet (12,077 square meters), the indoor farm will have a production output equivalent to 39.2 million square feet (3.6 million square meters) of farmland. That's more than 300 times increase in productivity.[5]

The rise of climate controlled farming methods like hydroponics are allowing indoor vertical farms to change the very constructs of how and where we produce food. Vertical farms are paving the way for the shift of the farm from rural field agriculture to high-tech, climate-controlled urban agriculture. Ultimately, vertical farming offers a completely novel way of farming that could feed people better.

FROM FIELD AGRICULTURE
TO INDOOR FARMING

Since the beginning of life on earth, food has traditionally been grown in soil, on large plots of land in the countryside or the outskirts of cities. In essence, the productive output of a farm is at the mercy of external environmental factors like temperature, sunlight, and rainfall. A cold spring season with minimal sunlight and excessive rainfall? A farmer's asparagus and green bean plants would barely sprout. Even in tropical climate countries like India, adverse weather events like droughts are detrimental to a farm's productive output.

At the start of the 20th century, farmers began searching for ways to make field agriculture less susceptible to external environmental factors. First, farmers protected their crops by placing small boxes with a flat glass roof over their crops. Overtime, these boxes transformed into the greenhouses we know of today, with farmers able to control the temperature and carbon dioxide levels in a greenhouse.[6] With these developments, agriculture became much more efficient and crop yields improved drastically.

However, agricultural ingenuity didn't stop there—technological innovations such as hydroponics and artificial lighting further optimized growing conditions and ultimately paved the way for indoor farming to emerge. Plant scientists and technologists concluded that rather than trying to control plants to fit the environment, they would adjust the environment to meet a plant's needs.[7] This shift in mentality led to the development of controlled indoor farming systems where the environment and agricultural inputs like light were optimized to a plant's needs. This method of using technology to grow crops indoors in a controlled and optimized environment is called Controlled Environment Agriculture (CEA).

Yet, that still wasn't enough for farmers and plant scientists. Eventually, the search for greater efficiencies in agriculture led to growing crops in vertically stacked layers. This is known as indoor vertical farming, a term coined by Columbia emeritus professor and author of *The Vertical Farm: Feeding the World in the 21st Century* Dickson Despommier.[8] He refers to this method of growing crops as "usually without soil or natural light, in beds stacked vertically inside a controlled-environment building."[9]

The core idea behind it is simple—to optimize agricultural inputs in order to grow as many crops as possible with the least amount of land. If it wasn't already obvious, vertical farming is much more productive than field farming. In the case of Emirates' and Crop One's vertical farm, technically only 1 acre in the vertical farm is required to produce 302 acres worth of crop output in traditional field agriculture. It's a wildly optimistic claim, but Bowery Farming, the U.S.-based indoor farm company with commercial vertical farms just outside New York City, has revealed that 1 square foot in one of its vertical farms is at least 100 times more productive than 1 square foot of arable land.[10] Even if the size of productivity gains is contentious, the main point is that vertical farming is clearly much more productive than conventional horizontal farming.

Looking towards 2050, the effects of climate change resulting in increasing temperatures and severe weather fluctuations demands that we look for novel ways of producing our food. With land loss, pesticide overuse, and soil degradation also being serious, global issues, indoor vertical farming is an optimal solution to the scarcity of fertile land. Ultimately, indoor vertical farming presents a highly attractive model for our future food production system.

There are three main types of indoor growth systems used in vertical farming:

1. **Hydroponics**—a form of soilless growing where the cultivation of plants occurs in an aquatic-based environment. In these soilless, water-based growth systems, a nutrient solution is pumped into reservoirs that plant roots grow directly into.[11]

2. **Aquaponics**—a growing system that integrates fish farming (aquaculture) and soil-free agriculture (hydroponics). Plants are grown in aquatic environments with nutrients coming from the waste of aquatic animals.

3. **Aeroponics**—an air-based growing system where plants grow not in a base of soil or water, but where a water and nutrient solution is sprayed directly onto roots for absorption.[12]

In this chapter, we'll dive deeper into hydroponics and aquaponics and how they play a role in the development of vertical farms that are re-imagining our cities. Considering such controlled farming systems are immune to external environment factors and are immensely more productive, the vertical farm is set to become the future farm that ensures better food security for the 10 billion people living on earth by 2050.

HYDROPONICS: WHERE'S THE SOIL?

While the concept of hydroponic growing has been around for thousands of years, the term "hydroponics" was first coined by Dr. William Gericke, a plant scientist at the University of California Berkeley, in 1937.[13] Gericke was utterly obsessed with growing plants in liquid. He was so obsessed that he started growing plants using nutrient solution culture in his backyard (The University of California Berkeley denied Gericke the use of the university's greenhouses due to the administration's skepticism, claiming it was a waste of taxpayers' money).[14]

Gericke made headlines when he managed to grow 25-feet (7.6m) high tomato vines and 12-feet (3.7m) high tobacco plants using only mineral nutrient solutions.[15] His initial prototype involved the plant's roots dipping into nutrient solution through wood wool and peat resting on wire netting.[16] Lined with redwood tanks, his backyard was the subject of many onlookers gazing with amazement at the concept of soilless growing. Gericke's backyard experiments would soon launch an evolution in farming.

Over the next few years, Gericke's work influenced the first commercial use of hydroponics and kick started the rise of commercial hydroponic growing. Convinced of Gericke's nutrient-solution based crops, Pan-Am Airways started a hydroponic garden at its important Wake Island base in 1939. A small island in the Pacific Ocean, Wake Island is a sandy, barren land devoid of sufficient soil and water for conventional farming. With the help of one of Gericke's students, Lamory Laumeister, tanks of mineralized water were used to grow beans, tomatoes, and vegetables.[17] The island was used as a refueling stop for Pan-Am Airways, and the food grown there successfully fed the airline's staff and crew for many years. During World War II, hydroponics was further used to grow crops for troops on barren Pacific Islands.[18]

When we think of farming, we think of crops and soil. Growing plants without soil and in a water-based system seems contrary to the traditional notion of plants needing nutrients from soil. In reality, all plants need to thrive is simply sunlight, water, and nutrients. As Gericke's work and Pan-Am Airways' operations have shown us, plants can also absorb nutrients through means beyond the soil substrate.

Today, the combination of human ingenuity and technological advancements like the Internet of Things has drastically advanced commercial hydroponic farming since Gericke's experiments in the 1930s. As of 2018, hydroponic farming is a global US$7.9 billion business,[19] and is projected to reach US$12.1 billion by 2025.[20] Dominated by Europe, hydroponic crop farming has gained in popularity due to its multitude of benefits and the instability of traditional farming methods impacted by poor weather conditions.

One of the biggest upsides of hydroponics is that it helps farmers reduce wastage and optimize the use of water and nutrients. Think back to barren Wake Island. Even though attempts were made to transport sufficient soil onto the island, there just wasn't enough water at Wake. At the time, hydroponic farming was highly attractive because it required less than a tenth of the water needed in soil farming.[21] In fact, some hydroponic crops use 90% less water than crops grown in soil.[22] For example, it can take as many as 34 gallons of water to produce a head of lettuce, but Plantagon, an indoor vertical farm in Sweden, can produce a head of lettuce using only about 0.25 gallons of water.[23]

The rationale behind this insane reduction is that in indoor hydroponic systems, water is often recycled and reused in the same system, leading to lower water costs and use. Thus, no water is lost except for water that transpires from the leaves; meanwhile, a traditional soil system would have elements like heat and soil salinity affecting the uptake of water by plants.

In hydroponics, precision technology also gives plants exactly the correct amounts of nutrients, water, and light it needs to thrive. This has enabled some crops to grow twice as fast in hydroponic systems compared to soil-based systems, where growing conditions aren't always optimal. Furthermore, hydroponic crops can grow in every season (even during heavy winters!), with crop growing cycles constantly restarting without the need to plow a soil field. That's a massive boost in growing time and therefore productivity for farmers.

In a future wrought with uncertain environmental conditions, hydroponics is a revolutionary solution in our quest to feed 10 billion people efficiently by 2050. There is no doubt that the mass utilization of hydroponic farming systems will play an immense role in the future of food production.

AQUAPONICS: TWO FOOD SOURCES, ONE SYSTEM

Building upon hydroponics, aquaponics is an emerging farming method that combines hydroponics and aquaculture (the farming of fish). The first forms of aquaponics had its roots in paddy fields in South China and Southeast Asia. The cultivation of rice in paddy fields coupled with fish swimming in paddy rivers brought about the novel idea of polyculture systems. Since then, floating aquaponics systems on fish ponds have been adopted in China on a large scale, with installations exceeding 10,000 square meters (2.5 acres).[24]

The most important aspect that aquaponics promotes is a highly sustainable, closed-loop system. In this system, fish grow in indoor ponds and the fish's nutrient-rich waste acts as a food source for growing plants; the plants then absorb the nutrients and biologically filter the water back into the fishponds for reuse. The system inherently recycles water, with fish and vegetables grown simultaneously in one controlled system without growth hormones, fertilizers, or pesticides.[25] That's a pretty damn productive system. It's like when I see people at the gym watch Netflix while working out—you kill two birds with one stone. In this case, you grow two food sources with one system!

The benefits brought by aquaponics are astounding. While requiring 90% less land and water than soil-based agriculture, it has the potential to produce 3 to 4 times the amount of food than in traditional agriculture.[26] With all natural fertilizers from fish waste, there is zero reliance on chemical fertilizers, making it a highly clean, sustainable, and efficient form of food production.

Moreover, farming more fish instead of other meat sources is incredibly beneficial to feeding our world; fish is currently one of the most resource-efficient ways to produce protein, as it requires less feed to produce the same mass of meat compared to land animals. Over a year, aquaponics can generate about 35,000 pounds (15,876 kg) of edible meat per acre, while grass-fed beef can only generate about 75 pounds (34 kg) in the same space.[27]

At a time when there's a labor scarcity in agriculture, both hydroponics and aquaponics offer incredibly self-sustaining solutions. These new farming systems are extremely low maintenance, since they do not require the same amount of human upkeep that traditional farms do. They are typically in compact spaces and have easier harvesting and replanting processes (there is no need for digging or weeding). In other words, when we build a smart, self-sustaining hydroponic or aquaponic farm, then, by default, we build a less labor-intensive farm.

In a resource-constraint and ever-changing climate future, hydroponic and aquaponic farming are highly attractive models that optimize resource use. On top of that, the risks of nutrient/fertilizer run-off and the infestation of pests and diseases are diminished with such systems. In the case of aquaponic systems, it means we can produce not just plant produce, but also fish protein to sufficiently nourish the world. Inevitably, powerful plant factories with indoor hydroponics and aquaponics systems will soon become a bigger part of our agricultural landscape.

THE ADVENT OF URBAN FARMING

Cities are densely populated, inundated with buildings, and scarce in open land; logically, they are unsuitable for agriculture and plant cultivation. However, advances in technology are challenging that perception. Technological innovations like hydroponic and aquaponic systems are now allowing farmers to grow crops vertically in sky-high buildings instead of horizontally across large acres of land.

With vertical farming systems, farmers can now grow food in places where it was formerly difficult or impossible, and in volumes comparable to traditional farms. For example, abandoned urban spaces like old warehouses have been used as a means to grow food in cities. This approach to urban farming provides fresh produce to supermarkets and retailers with minimal transportation costs and the ability to bolster the local food supply scene.

A company pioneering the urban farming model is BrightFarms, an indoor farm startup on a mission to grow fresh local produce in communities where it is consumed. BrightFarms' indoor hydroponic farms are located in and around metropolitan areas, allowing it to quickly and efficiently eliminate the time, distance, and costs associated with traditional energy-sucking food supply chains. Compared with long-distance, field-grown produce, BrightFarms' produce uses 80% less water, 90% less land, and 95% less shipping fuel.[28]

While most salad leaves travel thousands of miles through distributors before arriving (almost slimy and limp) in grocery stores 6-7 days after harvest, BrightFarms delivers to local supermarkets and retailers within 24 hours of harvest.[29] Not only are there environmental gains, consumers like you and I gain too. By traveling fewer miles, urban-grown produce is fresher and has higher nutrient retention since the nutrients in produce starts to degrade post-harvest. Retailers also gain, as fresher produce with shorter harvest-to-shelf times means longer shelf life and less food waste. By bringing hydroponic systems to urban areas, BrightFarms is able to provide better produce at competitive prices, while also cutting out intermediaries throughout the harvest-to-consumer supply chain.

As BrightFarms' model has shown, the most fundamental driver of urban agriculture is its ability to provide fresh food near the people that consume it, thereby reducing food miles and building self-sufficient communities. The topic of food miles, the distance that food has to travel from where it is sourced and harvested to where it is consumed, is a wildly popular topic amongst environmentalists. Urban farms drastically minimize food miles, presenting a highly attractive solution to our biggest food production problems.

The reality is that our food frequently travels thousands of miles along carbon-emissions heavy supply chains. For instance, the air pollution caused by importing garlic from China into the U.S. is estimated to result in 156 school absences a year.[30] In our highly globalized economy, agricultural trade is a significant contributor to greenhouse gas emissions. Ultimately, urban farms allow us to reduce the carbon footprint of traditional food transportation in heavily polluting supply chains.

With rising hunger and growing urban populations, we're turning to urban agriculture in the form of indoor vertical farming in and around cities in order to sufficiently nourish local populations. As indoor farming technology becomes more precise, the future will see farmers producing food in urban environments with minimal space and using far less water than on a conventional farm. And in a world of rapid climate change, indoor farming provides a highly controlled method of farming to mitigate extreme weather conditions.

"Urban agriculture may be critical to survival or a necessary adaptation to a changing climate," said researchers from a 2018 study led by Arizona State University and Google.[31] By analyzing multiple datasets in Google Earth Engine, a platform for processing geographical data, the study's researchers found that urban agriculture could save energy equivalent to the use of air conditioners in nearly 9 million U.S. households, and to produce up to 180 million tonnes of food.[32] Ultimately, it was concluded that urban farms could supply almost the entire recommended consumption of vegetables for city dwellers, while cutting food waste and reducing emissions from the transportation of agricultural products.[33]

From a food security, food quality, and environmentally conscious point of view, it just makes intuitive sense for us to grow food short distances from where we consume it. Placing farms close to supermarkets and consumers not only means better quality produce, it also means food can reach tables with less reliance on greenhouse-gas heavy transportation. The environmental and efficiency gains from indoor vertical farming is undeniably making way for such novel farming systems in the future of agriculture.

BARRIERS TO VERTICAL FARMING

Louis Albright, emeritus professor at Cornell University who helped pioneer controlled-environment agriculture, estimated that it would cost about US$23 per loaf of bread to pay the electricity bill (at US$0.10 per kilowatt-hour) for wheat grown in an indoor farm.[34] Currently, we pay an average of US$2.50 for a loaf of bread.[35]

Currently, urban vertical farms don't make economic sense for all types of crops. The overwhelming capital and energy costs associated with vertical farms is one of the biggest barriers to its mass adoption. The use of artificial LED lighting in indoor farms and the energy required to heat indoor farms means that the high energy costs of an indoor farm do not always justify its benefits.

Considering this, indoor farming is simply not commercially viable for low-value, staple crops like corn, soybeans, and rice. The low prices and thin profit margins of these commodity crops make it hard to justify the high costs of maintaining an indoor farm. As Paul P.G. Gauthier, a vertical farming expert at the Princeton Environmental Institute, points out, "We'll probably never grow soybeans, wheat, or maize indoors."[36]

Despite being unsuitable for low-value crops like corn and soybeans, vertical farming definitely makes sense for high-value, nutrient-dense crops like leafy greens, small fruits, herbs, and microgreens, on which many indoor farms have focused. The adoption of vertical farms in growing nutrient-dense foods like tomatoes and kale is steering the food system in the right direction. Growing more of these nutrient-dense crops is desperately needed to nourish the world by 2050. As the productivity of vertical farms drives down the costs of cultivating nutrient-dense crops, these foods will eventually become more affordable (and therefore accessible) for consumers. Furthermore, as companies like BrightFarms brings the farm closer to where we consume food, the reduced financial and environmental costs of transporting produce will also give consumers greater accessibility to these foods.

Apart from cost limitations, critics have also argued that the indoor vertical farm model uses and wastes an incredible amount of energy, resulting in a giant carbon footprint. Louis Albright estimates that the carbon emissions generated by growing 4,000 heads of lettuce in an indoor farm would be equivalent to the annual emissions of a passenger car.[37] That's pretty alarming. However, if you offset that with the significant reductions in land and water usage in indoor farms, the increased yield gains, and the reduced emissions from carbon-heavy supply chains, indoor farming models could well be justified.

There's a concern for heavy carbon emissions, but the big issue lies in energy wastage. It is estimated that only 1% of the artificial LED light supplied to plants is used in photosynthesis, while the remaining energy escapes as heat.[38] That is incredibly inefficient. Thus, finding ways to recycle and reuse wasted energy will be critically important for the sustainability of indoor vertical farms. With innovative ways of thinking, reusing this wasted energy is possible. Plantagon, the aforementioned Swedish indoor farm, re-directs 70% of escaped heat to warm the building above its

65,000 square foot farm.[39] Oxygen produced by the crops is also pumped into the building's air conditioning system. Evidently, Plantagon has built an efficient circulating system with minimal energy wastage. Its circular system also makes it a much more attractive prospect for landlords who save on energy costs.[40]

Despite these claims, it is important to note that many of these cost estimates arise only from indoor farms in countries that experience harsh, cold winters. The need to heat these indoor farms amidst cold environments results in significant energy usage levels and costs. However, in tropical countries like India and Singapore where almost no energy is expended to heat indoor farms, the energy costs are confined to lighting, making it a highly attractive farming system.

URBAN FARMS: SERVING ELITES OR THE FOOD INSECURE?

Often, the urban vertical farm industry is accused of serving only elite markets, rather than food insecure and malnourished communities that may not exist in major urban areas. The main concern is that the costs associated with urban farms are often unsuitable models for alleviating food deserts (communities that lack sufficient access to healthy food in the form of supermarkets or farmer's markets) located outside cities. That begs the question: will urban farm produce only exist to serve high-end consumers? It's a very valid concern often overlooked in discussions on sustainable food systems.

While more people are moving to cities, there will still be people living in rural areas and they risk facing even greater food insecurity as access to food diminishes. However, rather than hinder, indoor vertical farms can actually alleviate underserved communities like food deserts. A great example is Urban Organics, a company that operates urban aquaponic farms based in St. Paul, Minnesota. Since opening its first farm inside a former brewery complex in 2014, Urban Organics has brought food where it's needed most—to people in the food deserts of the Twin Cities of Minnesota, one of the worst U.S. states for food deserts.[41]

Urban Organics' second aquaponic farm in Minnesota could provide more than 124,700 kilograms (about 275,000 pounds) of fresh fish and nearly 215,500 kilograms (more than 475,000 pounds) of produce to the nearby area each year.[42] While contributing a significant amount of food in a comparatively small space, the integration of indoor farms in these areas also serve to revitalize them. Not only is Urban Organics providing good-paying, quality jobs for people in the area, it is also uplifting these developing communities, with new condominiums and even a food hall popping up in the area.

What Urban Organics has shown is that the indoor vertical farming model is not only confined to the city. In fact, the nature of food deserts being areas where food production has traditionally failed to thrive makes it hungry for a novel farming system that works anytime and anywhere. In this way, indoor vertical farms could effectively nourish, instead of neglect, these food insecure communities.

THE NETHERLANDS: THE FARM TECHNOLOGY POWERHOUSE

A small, densely populated country, the Netherlands is really bereft of almost all resources necessary for large-scale agriculture. Yet, it's the world's second highest exporter of food (in value), second only to the United States, which has 270 times its landmass. The Dutch are also the world's top exporter of potatoes and onions, as well as being the second largest exporter of vegetables overall.[43]

As if that wasn't impressive enough, it's also a world leader in tomato production, yielding more tomatoes per square mile than any other country on earth. Shockingly, it does this with the lowest water footprint in tomato production, using only 1.1 gallons per pound of tomatoes compared to the global average of 25.6 gallons per pound.[44] How on Earth have the Dutch done it? By being early pioneers of extraordinarily efficient climate-controlled farming methods like hydroponics.

Using cutting-edge methods from the highly acclaimed Wageningen University Research (WUR), the Dutch have successfully constructed self-contained food systems with a near-perfect balance between human ingenuity and nature's potential.[45] Without a doubt, this tiny country has become the world's agricultural powerhouse by using innovative technology to show the world what the future of farming will look like.

As we look to the future of farming, the Netherlands is a star example of a country that has successfully leveraged indoor farming technology to pioneer innovative solutions in sustainable agriculture. Yet, while the Netherlands has seen significant success, the same method of farming in the Netherlands may not work for other countries.

A ONE-SIZE-DOES-NOT-FIT-ALL SOLUTION

While hydroponic and aquaponic systems will play an integral role in the future of urban agriculture, it is definitely not a one-size-fits-all solution. Agriculture is a complex industry and that means different regions will need different solutions. In countries like Singapore and Japan, where land is a constraint but water is relatively available, hydroponics and aquaponics makes a lot of sense. However, in water-scarce nations like Israel and West Africa, hydroponics requires a different approach.

For several years now, Israel has suffered from a chronic water deficit.[46] Considering this, purely water-based hydroponics and aquaponics wouldn't work for Israel; it simply requires too much precious water—a resource it barely has. So instead of traditional soil-based agriculture, Israel uses a mineral substrate called vermiculite as the growing medium for its hydroponic systems.[47] One of Israel's most prominent innovations, vermiculite gives quick anchorage to roots, promoting faster root growth. It also has the ability to ration water release, minimizing water usage and preserving nutrient levels in plants.[48] When you're a country with one of the highest water shortages in the world, you're forced to innovate and adapt to ensure long-term water security.

Over in a tiny country like Singapore, land is extremely scarce but water is relatively abundant (Singapore sources its water from neighboring Malaysia). An island nation-state covering 720 km² or 278 square miles, the country is so small that less than 1% of its land is used for agriculture.[49] It's the reason why the country imports more than 90% of its food.[50] Let's just say the country isn't exactly self-sufficient.

With such limited space, the mentality in Singapore is always to "build high," not necessarily "build big." That makes it the perfect place for urban vertical farms that are much more space efficient. However, that's not nearly effective enough for Singapore. With so many high-rise buildings, even finding a decent piece of land with vertical space is a challenge. Therefore, urban farming has flocked to using rooftops for growing beds. For instance, organic farming company Citiponics operates "growing hydroponic towers" on multi-story car park rooftops.[51]

As Darren Ho, founder of Citizen Farm in Singapore, told me:

"You need to localize and contextualize it [technology-driven farming systems] to your country. A Dutch system in

a Dutch environment is different than putting a Dutch system in a Singapore environment."[52]

Over in neighboring Malaysia, my beloved home country, 24% of the country's land was used for agriculture in 2015.[53] While the state of Selangor produces 43% of the country's total food supply, it is reportedly short of agricultural land with only 12% available for farming.[54] With the state's rising population and rapid economic development, there is also the need for land for housing and new industries. While not completely scarce of land, novel farming systems like vertical farms are needed so that the lack of agricultural land in the state can be overcome.

Growing up in the state of Selangor, I remember drives to the airport where I would peer out the car window and cast my eyes at the vast palm oil estates that dominate the land. Since my family comes from the palm oil business, I knew growing up that these very estates were the lifeblood of my family. As I discovered the concept of vertical farming and the development of dwarf palm oil trees, I often wonder if palm oil trees can ever exist on a vertical farm. That would surely free up a lot more land desperately needed as Malaysia rapidly develops.

Evidently, indoor farming systems aren't a one-size-fits-all solution. It can take many forms and there is no one solution for every country. Different regions and countries have different needs; while land-scarce countries like Singapore may need hydroponic systems (albeit in a different way than how other countries deploy it), water-scarce countries like

Israel require adapted solutions. As we look into the future of an indoor farming era, we need to expand our approach and think beyond one fixed method. There are hundreds of forms of hydroponics—some heavily water-based and some mineral-based. The world really is our oyster.

THE FUTURE OF URBAN AGRICULTURE

Urban vertical farms will cause a drastic shift in the world's agricultural landscape. With advances in technology creating highly efficient indoor growing systems, no longer will agriculture be confined to the countryside or the outskirts of cities. The ancient practice of field farming will be revolutionized with modern technology, making agriculture more accessible, efficient, and productive than ever.

More importantly, vertical farming is allowing farmers to think about growing space in three-dimensional terms, instead of just two-dimensional. The transformational vertical farm model will be driven by the ability to produce greater yields in smaller areas, increase access to high quality produce, and reduce the environmental impacts of transporting food.

The future of urban agriculture will look like vertically stacked rows of growing racks lined with plants rooted in soil, nutrient-rich water, or air. Each row will have UV lights overlooking crops and self-sufficient water irrigation systems to maintain optimal water levels for crops. Soon, this is where our kale, Swiss chard, tomatoes, strawberries, herbs, and more will come from.

Cities as we know it will change forever. In the future, cities will see its food grown less than 10 miles away from where it is consumed. While we're probably not going to see superfarm cities where all farming happens in high-rise buildings, urban farms will undoubtedly become a part of future cityscapes. And as more data and evidence is released to show how urban farms directly benefit surrounding communities and the greater hunger epidemic, policy makers should be more compelled to support and invest in urban farms in the path to smarter and greener cities.

All this brings us to the final question: "Can indoor farming really help nourish the world?" Considering the cost limitations, it certainly isn't the only solution, but it is definitely part of the solution to solving the global hunger crisis. Pressing global issues like severe climate changes, soil degradation, land loss, and agrochemical pollution demands that we turn to novel ways of producing our food. It demands controlled climate farms that are defensible to extreme weather conditions. It demands a way of farming that takes pressure off the land and greatly reduces the contamination of water and soil through agrochemical runoff.

Dickson Despommier, the aforementioned vertical farm pioneer, says it better than I can: "Nature will repair itself if you give it a chance, and indoor farming gives it that chance."[55]

CHAPTER 5

SMART MICRO-GARDENS: THE DEMOCRATIZATION OF FOOD PRODUCTION

———

Tired of killing your garden patch or houseplant in a matter of weeks? Tired of bringing home a bunch of fresh basil and finding it, 4 days later, brown, wilted, and slimy? Tired of large corporations controlling every part of our food system? Meet the smart micro-garden—the next home appliance bringing plant power galore to your home.

I sit in my living room in Ithaca, New York, where it is currently -2°C (28°F) and snowing outside. I stare out my window and from the corner of my eye, I spot two mini plant pots sitting on my windowsill. Sure, there is soil in the pots, but no vegetation is in sight—not in this weather at least. All that remains in the soil, are the shriveled-up root remains from the basil and rosemary plants that used to be there.

Like many, I do not live in a house that has a massive garden. And to be honest, even if I did, my basil and rosemary plants would definitely not survive this weather. Also, who is going to water my plants when I leave New York to go home to Malaysia for a while? I would probably need someone to babysit my plants. Clearly, there's a problem with trying to grow food at home.

Enter home growing systems or what I like to call smart micro-gardens. Smart, technology-driven, mini machines that seamlessly give plant life to your home.

One such plant machine is SproutsIO, an automated indoor growing system that allows you to grow crops at home. The SproutsIO machine consists of a basin, where a nutrient solution circulates around the plant roots and sensors monitor key environmental factors such as pH and temperature.[1] Atop the basin, are seedpods where you can grow produce like kale, chili peppers, and fairy tale eggplant. Fitted with an overhead lamp, onboard cameras, and environmental sensors, SproutsIO allows you to adjust the intensity of light, mist your plants, and receive real-time reports on your plant's growing status, all with a click of the SproutsIOGrow app.

Yes, an app on your digital device that lets you have a peek of your plants and maintain the growing conditions of your produce. With a machine like SproutsIO, you can grow plants at home without even living at home. How crazy is that?

IoT enablement and innovative design systems thinking has given rise to a wave of smart micro-gardens such as SproutsIO. Like the indoor farming technologies discussed in Chapter 4, the real power of such machines is that machine learning allows it to learn from growing experience and optimize growing conditions. After all, growing crops is not a simple task; small changes in temperature, pH, humidity, light, and soil acidity can make a massive difference in crop growth. Smart micro-gardens like SproutsIO not only adjusts the system to create ideal conditions for your crops, it also helps you build crop conditions that grow sweeter kale or juicier tomatoes.[2]

The arrival of home growing systems is ushering in a new generation of innovators creating the next home appliance. Whether it uses hydroponics with a nutrient solution or aquaponics with a fish tank, such home growing systems are increasing access to growing food at home. It's giving consumers the power to produce some of their food and the power to connect with where their food comes from.

Just as vertical farming is bringing the farm to cities, smart micro-gardens are bringing a part of the farm to our homes. This is wildly significant, because the kind of self-sufficient plant power offered by such home growing systems is far from our current tightly controlled food system. For the first time in centuries, every consumer can finally have a say in a local food system we desperately want and need.

CORPORATE CONTROL OF OUR FOOD

Today, our food system is powered by a handful of companies that decide everything from the market price that farmers get for their crops to the types of herbicides used on crops. While we seemingly have myriad choices available to us in the supermarket, the reality is that only a few large multinational companies dictate the food we eat. Four major companies—Kellogg's, General Mills, Post, and Quaker—dominate 80-90% of the cereal market.[3] Just three companies—Monsanto, DuPont, and Syngenta—control 55% of the global seed market.[4]

How did our food system become the definition of inequality? The answer: corporate-favoring policies and merger mania in the food industry. A lack of government antitrust intervention has allowed significant consolidation in the agri-food industry. Consequently, the lack of competition has permitted giant seed and biotechnology companies to control the market price that farmers get for their crops.[5] Furthermore, they have the power to increase the price of inputs and ultimately drive down farmer income.

"Mergers are set to re-shape world farming, potentially raising prices for growers and consumers around the world," says Adrian Bebb, Senior Food, Agriculture and Biodiversity Campaigner for Friends of the Earth Europe.[6]

"From Africa and Asia to Latin America and the EU, corporate control over markets and supply chains is displacing millions of small-scale farmers. These dynamics have created some of the world's highest rates of poverty and hunger among small-scale food producers and rural communities worldwide," urges Bebb.[7]

By concentrating market control and access to big data, patents, seeds, and land among a few corporations, millions of smallholder farmers, which make up over 90% of farmers worldwide, are at risk of losing their livelihoods.[8] With concentrated political, financial, and research power in the hands of a small group of powerful agricultural input companies, smallholders have inevitably been stepped on, competition has significantly stifled, and farm input prices have consequently risen.[9]

All this agri-business consolidation happens concurrently with the consolidation of the world's major food producers.[10] Large multinationals like Tyson, Nestlé, and General Mills have the power to produce more unhealthy processed food at dipping costs. With their immense influence, these companies have the power to propagate the use of factory farms, engage in environmentally damaging farming practices and even greenwash consumers into thinking that the food on our shelves are "all natural." Clearly, tight corporate control of our food system is harming consumers, farming communities, the environment, and ultimately, our democracy.

Our current food and agricultural system is inherently not democratic. It is a global problem with its roots planted deep in corporate control of our food system. As consumers, we are forced to rely on the "expert knowledge" of food manufacturers and their carefully crafted labels in order to decide what to eat. As consumers, we are forced to accept that most produce we buy on the market today has been treated with a multitude of chemicals despite the deceptive label of "organic." As consumers, we are relegated to a corner of the food system that large agri-food corporations want us to be exposed to and ignorant to what happens behind closed doors. Is this what we want for the future of our food system?

FIGHTING FOR FOOD SOVEREIGNTY

How can we take back control of our food system? How can we snatch back the tight reins that large corporations have on our food?

That's where the idea of food sovereignty emerged. Food Sovereignty asserts that people who directly produce and consume food (namely farmers and consumers) should be able to control the mechanisms and policies of food production and distribution, instead of the intermediary corporations that have come to dominate our global food system.[11] The idea is that by reducing or even removing the control that large corporations have in producing our food, we can have a bigger say in how our food is produced and distributed.

In the fight for food sovereignty, promoting local food systems by buying directly from farmers is a big part of the solution. Going to farmers markets and buying from the very people who have grown our food is truly a life-changing experience. Not only do we have greater assurance that the food we are buying is of a high quality, but we also have a greater sense of purpose and trust in the food system by developing relationships with food producers. Ultimately, creating authentic, direct relationships with the people who produce our food brings us closer to food sovereignty and ultimately, a food democracy. But growing our own food brings us even closer.

In the future, smart micro-gardens like SproutsIO will give us greater control over our food system, allowing us to return to some degree of growing our own food. With technological innovations in climate-controlled growing systems, the advent of smart home growing systems is allowing consumers to easily grow produce at home anytime, anywhere.

For the first time in history, the limitations on our knowledge, limitations on yield, and most importantly, limitations on climate can no longer stop us from growing food at home. Of course, it is silly to argue that we should go back to a subsistence farming system and grow all of our own food. In fact, economics dictates that it is optimal for us to have farms that specialize in growing certain crops, but the simple act of growing some vegetables and herbs at home gives us a little more control over what we put into our bodies. It gives us a better understanding of where our food comes from. It gives us a sense of mindfulness and fulfillment from growing our own food. It purifies and oxygenates the air we breathe and most importantly, it improves our relationship with nature—a relationship that has long been neglected and arguably, destroyed.

BARRIERS TO SMART MICRO-GARDEN ADOPTION

Like all things involving change, there are challenges to the adoption of smart micro-gardens. Most notably, price is a significant barrier. The SproutsIO system sounds great, but it costs a whopping US$799.[12] The EcoGarden, a micro-aquaponics system that combines a self-cleaning fish tank and a smart micro-garden, costs US$290.[13] While the smart micro-gardens on the market range in price, one thing is certain—they aren't yet affordable for everyone. It is important to note that the advancements made in indoor farming technology are relatively recent. Thus, the technology is currently only cost-efficient when deployed at scale like in the vertical farms discussed in Chapter 4; this makes the development of micro-garden systems particularly time and cost-consuming.

However, as we've seen with other home appliances, the price of devices often plummets over time. Take the Amazon Echo for example. Its initial introductory price was

US$179.99.[14] Today, you can buy it for less than 40% of that price at US$69.99.[15] Previous home devices have shown us that as sales volume increases and the costs of sensing and information technologies decreases, smart micro-gardens like SproutsIO and the EcoGarden will similarly experience significant price decreases. The road to commercialization is never easy, but the technology to create highly advanced micro-gardens is there; time and scale are now the remaining issues. With a heavy emphasis on usability and design of these plant machines, we can ultimately make these devices highly accessible, attractive, and functional for consumers and bring it into the mainstream by 2050.

Another barrier for mass adoption is that such advanced IoT enablement is currently not easily accessible in less developed parts of the world. While this is true, these smart micro-garden systems are created deliberately to be highly accessible to regions where mobile phone penetration has experienced significant growth. Countries like China, India, and Kenya have incredible rates of mobile penetration, deeming them suitable stakeholders to develop and adopt such connected growing systems for the home.

A DEMOCRATIC FUTURE FOOD SYSTEM

In a democratized food world, smart micro-gardens will help bring a part of our food system into our hands and into our homes. Just as we have the Amazon Alexa at home and smart crock pots with auto timers, imagine having an Apple product minimalistic, portable plant machine, capable of growing food at home. Imagine picking your spinach or rosemary right from the comfort of your home. You'd best believe it. In the future, smart micro-gardens will allow us to grow produce at home and increase our level of self-sufficiency. It will mean that we can grow some of our own food and reduce the need to rely on large corporations for our food.

While currently not mainstream, having a plant machine at home is really not far in the future. In 2016, IKEA already introduced a line of indoor gardening systems and accessories that allow people to grow their own lettuce and herbs anytime of the year.[16] Since 2017, we've seen a wave of home growing systems like SproutsIO and Click and Grow enter the market, but the price and accessibility to such systems is still a challenge facing mass adoption. However, as technological advances and scale is achieved, it's only a matter of time before such smart plant machines become as ubiquitous as the countertop coffee machine.

The future of the home appliance lies in smart micro-gardens like SproutsIO. Such growing systems are spearheading the future of democratizing our food system. It's spearheading the future of giving us some power in how our food is grown, transported, and consumed.

PART III

RE-ENGINEERING
OUR FOOD

CHAPTER 6

GMOS: THE FORBIDDEN HERO

———

Love it or hate it, genetically modified organisms (GMOs) are integral to building highly resilient crops. Think drought-tolerant soybeans that can withstand long, grueling droughts. Think corn plants that are indifferent to pest damage and soil-borne diseases. The future of agriculture demands that we turn to GMOs in our fight against climate change.

Genetically Modified Organisms. GMOs. Did you just flinch? I don't blame you, they get a bad rep. A really, really bad one. They have faced large-scale condemnation with an upheaval of GMO critics in the last 20 years. They are dubbed "Frankenfoods" by consumers terrified of eating blueberries genetically enriched with antioxidants or avocados with an anti-browning gene. They're painted as the villain in the consumer food product world, with large corporations actively acquiring "non-GMO" labels like they are "non-Halal" labels.

In fact, Mike Hoffman, executive director of the Cornell Institute for Climate Smart Solutions, told me that when he once went to the supermarket and was looking for a bag of chips, he couldn't find *a single bag* that wasn't labeled "non-GMO."[1] Trek down the supermarket aisle and you'll find very few foods with the label "Partially produced with genetic engineering,"—the result of a 2016 federal law mandating labels on all products containing genetically engineered ingredients.[2] Evidently, the non-GMO stance has become the gold standard in the consumer food world, and that might not be such a good thing for the future of our food and agricultural system.

Besides in indoor farms (discussed in Chapter 4), agriculture is undoubtedly highly dependent on the climate. Small increases in temperature or carbon dioxide (CO_2) in the atmosphere can have a major effect on crop yields. The reality is that climate change is making it incredibly difficult to grow crops in the same places and ways as before. The health of a crop depends on its optimum temperature, water, and nutrient needs in relation to its external environment.

One could say that growing a crop is very similar to making a cake. You mix together ingredients like butter, sugar, and flour, and by beating the batter to incorporate air and applying the right amounts of heat and moisture during baking, a beautiful, fluffy cake is produced. Turn the heat up too high and you'll end up with a cake burnt on the outside and uncooked on the inside. Add too little flour and you'll end up with a pudding instead of a cake. Crops are very similar. Slight changes in inputs like water and CO_2 and your crop is damaged. For example, according to the U.S. Environmental Protection Agency (EPA), premature budding due to a warm winter caused US$220 million in losses of Michigan cherries in 2012.[3]

Moreover, as global warming accelerates in the coming decades, researchers have found that rising global temperatures will lead to increased pest pressure on crops. "When the temperature increases, the insects' metabolism increases so they have to eat more. That's not good for crops," explains Scott Merrill, a researcher at the University of Vermont's Department of Plant and Soil Science and Gund Institute for Environment.[4] As the earth warms, the metabolic rate of insects will increase and their population growth will accelerate accordingly.

That's major bad news for the livelihood of our crops. Crop losses to insects are projected to rise by 10-25% per degree of warming in the future.[5] Even with the most optimistic global warming predictions, this means that crop losses to insects will increase by up to 25% by 2050. That is certainly not a positive future, considering we will need to increase food production by at least 50%, if we're going to stand a chance of nourishing almost 10 billion people by 2050.

Ultimately, climate change is driving the heavy fluctuation of the environment and inputs. Extreme events like severe drought and floods harm farmers and drastically reduce yield. Warmer temperatures and increased CO_2 levels help more weeds, pests, and fungi thrive. And as much as indoor farms will be central to the hunger agenda in the coming years, there is no guarantee that every part of the world will be able to afford and develop appropriate climate-controlled systems by 2050.

Hence, the genetic modification (GM) of seeds and crops will be a critical solution that will equip us with the tools we need to mitigate the risks of global warming.

CONVENTIONAL BREEDING VS. GENETIC MODIFICATION VS. GENE EDITING

Over the last decades, the tinkering of the genome of crops has taken multiple forms and methods. The terms genetic modification, gene editing, and selective/conventional plant breeding often incite confusion or misinterpretation. In essence, the goals of all three are to produce crops with improved and optimal characteristics by changing the genetic makeup of crops.

The earliest forms of gene-tinkering in crops is what we call selective or conventional plant breeding, which is the process of crossing the genes of two parent plants with relevant characteristics and selecting the offspring with the desired combination of characteristics.[6] Usually, this is done through artificially mating or cross-pollinating. Humans have been selectively breeding crops for centuries, breeding new and improved varieties of crops that have dramatically increased the productivity and quality of our crops.[7]

In many ways, conventional plant breeding is a precursor to the modern concept of genetic modification (GM). When the concept of DNA was discovered in the early 1900s and advancements in genetic techniques were developed in the 1970s, scientists started altering the gene of crops.[8] A wave of GMOs would soon ensue.

The differing ideologies of what constitutes a GMO make it a hard topic to discuss. Are GMOs just organisms that have had foreign genes directly added to its genome? Or is a GMO any organism that has had its genome modified or changed in any way? In the latter case, almost every plant we eat today has been genetically modified through selective and conventional breeding. Farmers and agricultural scientists have been "genetically modifying" our food for centuries, resulting in large exchanges of genetic material anyway. So why do we have so many non-GMO certified labels? Why couldn't Mike Hoffman find a damn bag of potato chips that isn't labelled "non-GMO"?

Globally, the most recent and widely used definition of GMOs is from the Codex Alimentarius, a collection of food standards and guidelines used by the World Health Organization (WHO) and the Food and Agriculture Organization (FAO) of the United Nations.[9]

According to the Codex Alimentarius, the following definitions of GMO are used:

"Living modified organism" means any living organism that possesses a novel combination of genetic material obtained through the use of modern biotechnology;[10]

"Modern biotechnology" means the application of:[11]

1. *In vitro nucleic acid techniques, including recombinant deoxyribonucleic acid (DNA) and direct injection of nucleic acid into cells or organelles, or*

2. *Fusion of cells beyond the taxonomic family, that overcome natural physiological reproductive or recombination barriers and that are not techniques used in traditional breeding and selection;*

The most common and colloquial definition of GMOs is that it involves the transfer of genes from one species to an entirely different species through human intervention. Basically, it is the act of adding a new gene or genes to the existing genome of a crop in order to introduce a new trait. For instance, genetically engineering pest resistance as a trait would involve physically inserting a gene from a bacterium into a maize crop so that the crop can create its own insecticide. These organisms containing foreign genetic material are also known as transgenic organisms and are what forms the basis of GMO crops.

Despite conventional breeding techniques, GM techniques emerged because interbreeding between completely different species and organisms just can't happen with traditional breeding techniques or in nature. The gene or trait of interest (e.g. pest resistance) does not always exist in the same species that can be successfully cross-bred through conventional breeding. Furthermore, the act of introducing foreign genes into a crop simply does not occur through evolution; certain genes don't come into contact with each other and even if they do by mistake, the chances of it being compatible enough to be expressed is slim.[12]

As opposed to conventional breeding and GM, gene editing is an emerging technique used to re-engineer crops. In gene editing, new plant traits are introduced by directly rewriting a crop's genetic code, instead of inserting a new gene. It is merely what its name suggests—editing the existing genome.

A huge incentive of using gene-editing technologies to create so-called "designer crops" is that the U.S. Department of Agriculture (USDA) does not regulate crop varieties developed through gene editing. Comparatively, crops that include genes from foreign organisms, like bacteria, is considered a GMO and is heavily regulated and repelled by consumers. This distinction has compelled many researchers and companies to prefer using gene-editing tools instead of genetic modification methods. A huge frontier in gene-editing technology is CRISPR, which stands for "Clustered Regularly Interspaced Short Palindromic Repeats."[13] We'll get more into why CRISPR will be the future of re-engineering our crops in Chapter 7.

THE GOLDEN RICE CONTROVERSY

One of the most valuable yet controversial products of genetic modification is Golden Rice. Golden Rice is a genetically modified, bio-fortified rice that produces beta-carotene, which is not naturally produced in rice and is converted into vitamin A when metabolized by the body.

First introduced in 1999 by two professors, Ingo Potrykus and Peter Beyer, Golden Rice was created to significantly increase the nutritional content of rice in order to combat the issue of vitamin A deficiency (VAD).[14] VAD is a severe public health problem affecting more than half the world, especially in developing countries in Africa and Asia. According to the World Health Organization, an estimated 250 million preschool children are vitamin A deficient; every year, up to 500,000 of these children become blind.[15] In fact, VAD is the leading cause of preventable blindness in children and women worldwide.

Considering the severity of VAD, Golden Rice was created to relieve the VAD epidemic. However, soon after the Golden Rice Project was announced, opposition to it formed and halted expansion of the project. Organizations like Greenpeace and Friends of the Earth argued against the project, stating that the project was flawed. Critics claimed that existing VAD solutions were cheaper and did not require

GMOs. Furthermore, they contended that the motives of the Golden Rice Project were questionable with possible ties to large biotech industries wanting to make a profit. It was even argued that the project was a ploy to increase public support of GMOs and take attention away from cheaper and more realistic solutions![16]

Many people strongly resisted GM crops even at the expense of solving a worldwide epidemic like VAD. Could Golden Rice have helped prevent up to 500,000 vitamin A deficient children from becoming blind every year? Probably. So why did we resist it? Part of it can be attributed to the perceived connection between GMOs and large biotech companies, which incited public distrust. Another part of it can be attributed to the human instinct of resisting significant change. After all, human nature compels us to fear the unknown.

In reality, the hindrance of the commercialization of golden rice was a missed opportunity for the benefit of humanity. Golden rice had concrete potential to drastically decrease VAD and reduce preventable blindness around the world. If we could only look past the labeling of GMOs as bad and embrace GMOs, we could actually uncover a new host of solutions to not only the VAD epidemic, but also other preventable micronutrient-related issues like iron deficiency.

Considering the severity of the global malnutrition problem, which affects about 2 billion people globally, genetic modification could play a central role in enhancing the nutritional value of commodity crops like rice and horticultural crops like bananas. With GM crops, we can actually produce food that meets our optimal health and nutrition needs, instead of just caloric needs. In other words, with GM crops, we could nourish the world.

GMOS IN THE FUTURE OF CLIMATE CHANGE

"One of the greatest paradoxes for me are people who reject GMOs yet accept the science of climate change," said Jan Nyrop, director of Cornell AgriTech and associate dean of the Cornell College of Agriculture and Life Sciences.[17]

When Jan told me this, it immediately made sense. Those who deny the use of GMOs are inherently on the same wavelength as those who refuse to accept the mainstream view of human-imposed climate change. Because if one is a believer in climate change, then surely one can see how genetic modification of crops to be more weather-resistant is a boon for our future. You see, GM crops are not just needed for a future wrought with climate change—they are strikingly necessary.

The primary way GMOs will help mitigate the effects of climate change is by increasing crop resilience. By applying GM techniques, scientists have created GM crop varieties that can withstand unpredictable climates and thrive on arid lands usually considered unsuitable for farming. If we can't grow all crops indoors and we can't halt climate change, then let's make crops more resilient to the external environment.

When I was in high school, I learned about non-renewable energy sources like fossil fuels in biology. Despite the world's major focus on the scarcity of fossil fuels, I distinctly remember my biology teacher Emma Campbell predict an impending water shortage. She said that the world is facing a fossil fuel crisis now, but 30 years from now, the world will face a great water crisis. Her prediction was pretty accurate. Throughout this book, the severity of droughts worldwide has been repeatedly emphasized. However, there's a solution—drought-resistant crops.

In areas like Southern Africa where rain is erratic and drought seasons are a regular occurrence, drought-resistant seeds have large implications for farmers. These seeds are incredibly water efficient and tolerant of water shortages for long periods of time. In Africa, the Drought Tolerant Maize for African Seed Scaling project (DTMASS) found that over a period of five years, 2.9 million farmers covered by the DTMASS project saw yields increase by 20% to 30% after sowing a variety of drought-tolerant seeds.[18]

Considering how unforeseeable our future climate will be, drought-resistance seeds like the ones deployed by DTMASS will become a key innovation for farming. Countries most vulnerable to climate change like West Africa and India are already poised to experience yield declines over the next three decades. In fact, the UN has predicted that yields in West Africa and India could fall by as much as 2.9% and 2.6% respectively by 2050 due to climate change.[19] With drought-resistant crops, farmers will not suffer invariably because of sudden changes in the weather. Put simply, a future with drought-resistant crops is a future that need not be afraid of sudden climate-induced drought.

As previously discussed, climate change is also set to accelerate the population of insects and pests harmful to crop production. By genetically engineering resistance to pest damage, food producers have been able to use fewer pesticides while significantly increasing yields. A meta-analysis of 150 studies published in the highly regarded journal PLOS One concluded that adoption of GMOs actually reduces chemical pesticide use by 37%, increases crop yields by 22%, and increases farmer profits by 68%.[20] Reduced use of pesticides not only enhances the safety of farmers and the environment, it also reduces the cost of crop inputs for farmers. Thus, being able to prevent future crop losses to pests will truly be a fundamental area where GMOs can add immense value.

David Rotman, editor of the *MIT Technology Review*, agrees: "Climate change will make it increasingly difficult to feed the world. Biotech crops will have an essential role in ensuring that there's enough to eat."[21] I couldn't have said it better myself.

With impending bouts of unpredictable climate changes, GM crops will become crucial for food production in the future. Advances in genetic modification will give us the ability to cultivate the most pest-resistant and drought-tolerant crops the world has seen. Ultimately, it will put us in a good position to meet the food and nutritional health demands of 10 billion people.

DEMYSTIFYING THE NEGATIVE GMO LABEL

In any supermarket or retailer, shelves upon shelves of food products bear the much sought-after butterfly emblem of the Non-GMO project—a symbol of purity and safety. The label has become as prevalent as the USDA Organic label in the consumer food product world, but behind it hides a string of anti-GMO hysteria.

Mark Lynas was one of the prominent activists of the anti-GMO movement. Back in the 1990s when GMOs were first introduced, he trespassed on farms to destroy test fields of GMO crops, organized the first major campaign vilifying Monsanto, protested for the ban of foods containing GMOs, and even attempted (unsuccessfully) to steal the world's first cloned farm animal—Dolly the Sheep.[22] However, in 2013, in a recantation speech, Lynas apologized for destroying GM crops.[23]

"I have since reversed my views on GMOs, as the evidence debunking almost all of these claims has accumulated over the years, but there's no denying the remarkable worldwide success of our campaign," he reveals in his Wall Street Journal expose "Confessions of an Anti-GMO Activist."[24] Lynas is so adamant about his change of view that he even published a book titled "*Seeds of Science: Why We Got It So Wrong on GMOs.*"

While Lynas has changed his mind, most people around the world still think that GMO foods are harmful for human health or likely to damage the environment. While it gets a bad reputation, GMOs are largely not fully understood by the public. In 2014, talk show host Jimmy Kimmel sent a reporter to a West Coast farmers market to ask shoppers what they thought of GMOs. While all the interviewees stated their strong avoidance of GMOs, they failed to even explain what the letters "GMO" stand for.[25] Do GMO critics even truly understand what a GMO is?

Perhaps the most common claim against GMOs is that it is damaging to human health and increases the risk of everything from diabetes to obesity to cancer. However, in the decades since GM foods were introduced, there has been a lack of concrete evidence to show direct correlations between GMOs and negative health effects. In fact, in 2015, the U.S. National Academy of Sciences (NAS) published a multi-year assessment of the safety of GM crops and found "no differences between GM crops and its conventionally grown counterparts that implicate a higher risk to human health safety."[26] There is simply an absence of credible long-term feeding studies to suggest that GMOs are harmful to human health.

The controversy and resistance of GMOs is really due to an incredible amount of misinformation in the public. There is ample scientific evidence to show that the genetic changes we are making are safe. Yet, there is a massive information gap between fact-based science and consumer perception. "The disjunction between scientific consensus and public opinion on the topic of GMOs is disturbing, to say the least," agrees Jennifer A. Doudna, author of *A Crack in Creation: Gene Editing and the Unthinkable Power to Control Evolution.*[27]

This information gap was clearly evident to me as I talked to plant scientists and researchers about their views on GMOs. All the scientists and researchers I spoke to believe that GMOs have no serious health concerns and are crucial for the future of food production. In fact, 90% of scientists believe GMOs are safe—a statement endorsed by the National Academy of Science, the American Medical Association, the American Association for the Advancement of Science and the World Health Organization—yet only slightly more than a third of consumers share this belief.[28] Why is there a distrust of science? And if there are no significant studies that show the negative impacts of GMOs on human health, then why do they have such a bad reputation?

"Everything is based on good science. The problems with GMOs have been how they've been implemented," offers Mike Hoffman, Executive Director of the Cornell Institute for Climate Smart Solutions.[29]

Hoffman is right. GMOs get a bad reputation amongst consumers largely because many GM crops on the market have been misused and exploited by large seed and biotechnology companies. Much like software companies have proprietary technology, these seed and biotechnology companies have patents to manage the use and distribution of their genetically modified seeds. Essentially, these companies have the power to sue farmers whose fields contain GMO crops that the farmer has not purchased in seed. In fact, the most notorious seed and biotechnology company, Monsanto, has sued many farmers and even has a hotline that people can call to alert them to patent infringements![30]

It's safe to say that the significant power these large biotechnology companies have in using GMOs have incited significant public distrust of GMOs. Furthermore, the inundation of public media platforms widely condemning GMOs has played a big role in hurting GMO's public reputation.

While GM crops have traditionally harmed farmer sovereignty, we can change that and put GMOs in a new light. By not limiting the uses of GM seeds to large agri-businesses, we can shift the power dynamics and make the genetic modification of crops highly accessible to all stakeholders. By not shunning the use of GMOs, we can soon discover that it is, in fact, a hidden and forbidden hero in agriculture.

In exploring the origins of GMO repulsion, it is reasonable to conclude that GMOs have a bad reputation not because there is *actual* scientific evidence that shows it is harmful, but because there is a great deal of *perceived* knowledge that it is bad. Meanwhile, the scientific community has known for years that there is no basis for the perceived negative implications of GMOs. The knowledge gap between the scientific community's consensus on GMOs and the public's misconception of GMOs is frankly alarming for the future of agriculture in a climate-uncertain future. We must act to demystify the label and act on good, real science.

"The anti-GMO campaign has deprived much of the world of a crucial, life-improving technology—and has shown the readiness of many environmentalists to ignore science when it contradicts their prejudices. That's not the example we need just now as the planet faces the very real threat of climate change," emphasizes Lynas, who upon reversing his negative views on GMOs, spent subsequent years working with plant scientists in Africa and Asia to help smallholder farmers in developing countries use GMOs to better cope with pests, diseases, and droughts.[31]

In an opinion piece for *Nature Biology*, Richard B. Flavell, a prominent British molecular biologist, warns about the dangers of vilifying and hindering GM technologies:

"The consequences of simply sustaining the chaotic status quo—in which GMOs and other innovative plant products are summarily demonized by activists and the organic lobby—are frightening when one considers mounting challenges to food production, balanced nutrition, and poverty alleviation across the world. Those who seek to perpetuate the GMO controversy and actively prevent use of new technology to crop breeding are not only on the wrong side of the debate, they are on the wrong side of the evidence."[32]

The anti-GMO campaign is perhaps one of the most successful international campaigns that is utterly misinformed and ironically not based on real science. If we're going to continue sustaining ourselves in an ever-changing future climate, we need to make way for these scientific changes.

PLAYING WITH NATURE

A rather subjective argument against GMOs is that critics insist we should not be "playing with nature" by experimenting with the building blocks of life. In truth, few transformative scientific advances are widely embraced at first. For example, immunologist James Allison's proposed use of immunotherapy to treat cancer was thoroughly rejected by biotech and pharmaceutical companies.[33] Today, it is heralded as a revolution in cancer treatment and Allison has produced some of the most clinically and commercially successful cancer drugs on the market.

Similarly, it is natural for GM crops to be met with initial—albeit strong—resistance before being embraced. As cancer immunotherapy drugs have shown, scientific discoveries soon proliferate once its impacts are widely felt, despite doubters and critics. If this was not the case, science would not have had great leaps throughout history and we would still be living a primitive existence.

Some fear playing with nature will in turn cause further harm to nature. GMOs are accused of causing significant environmental damage, because crops are being genetically modified to withstand weed killers, which would be excessively used. It is true that about 80% of all GM crops worldwide have been engineered for herbicide tolerance, allowing these crops to survive after herbicide treatment.[34] Just like the antibiotic-resistant bacteria crisis, critics claim that GMOs have caused a herbicide-resistant crop crisis. This is not entirely true, because while the use of toxic herbicides did increase sixteen-fold since the mid-1990s (when GMOs were introduced), the increase is not solely due to GM crops developing a strong resistance to herbicides.[35] There are many other reasons for why herbicide use has increased. For one, the increased cultivation of commodity crops in developing nations saw more farmers discovering the use of herbicides as a way to combat weeds.

Contrary to the claims against GMOs, GM crops have actually been able to dramatically reduce the amount and toxicity of pesticides used. Crops like Bt corn, which incorporate proteins toxic to insects from the bacterium *Bacillus thuringiensis,* have allowed farmers to reduce the use of both insecticides and herbicides. There's direct evidence to show it. The aforementioned meta-analysis of 150 studies from the prominent journal PLOS One revealed that due to GM crops' internal biological protection against insects and weeds, GM crops used 37% less chemical pesticides (both insecticide and herbicide) compared with conventional versions of the same crops.[36]

Mark Lynas, the previous anti-GMO activist turned GMO proponent, adds that pesticide reductions are even more notable in developing countries. During his time in Bangladesh working with farmers, he saw firsthand how smallholder farmers have benefited from Bt varieties of eggplant. Before Bt eggplant, they would spray their crops with toxic agrochemicals as many as 100 times per season to fight off harmful pests and weeds. With GMO eggplant, Lynas observed how farmers dramatically reduced insecticide spraying, in some places reducing spraying almost to zero.[37]

GMO's supposed environmental damages purported by critics are often exaggerated and extrapolated without concrete evidence. Again, there is a gap between good science and consumers. Trusting substantial scientific evidence, instead of ill-informed ideologies, is the only way we'll embrace technological and scientific innovations that will help solve our most pressing food production problems. Furthermore, the fear of meddling with nature is a non-progressive one at best. After all, humanity didn't get this far without believing in positive changes that new technologies can bring.

THE GMO VERDICT

In the next three decades, we simply cannot nourish 10 billion people using low-productivity methods of the past. Historical agricultural discoveries like the production of artificial fertilizers and the discovery of dwarf wheat varieties have helped humanity nearly eliminate mass famine. Similarly, in the future, we must not hinder promising food technologies like GMOs because of ill-informed cries of fear.

If you're wary of or even against GMOs, I get it. Genetic modification sounds sinister and conjures up images of mutant fruit and vegetables that will result in unconceivable consequences if consumed. However, many of us have been fed information that has failed to be backed by good science.

The verdict is out—science has proven repeatedly that GMOs are not dangerous for human consumption.

Despite the misuse of GMOs by large agri-businesses, GMOs are the reason that we've been able to sustain high crop yields to feed the world, enhance the nutritional content of our produce, and increase crop resilience to mitigate the effects of climate change. Especially with the looming future of unpredictable weather changes, GM crops will become even more vital in the fight for our survival on earth. Moreover, the technology hasn't even reached its potential. So far, large-scale pest-resistant crops have commonly only been modified to include the Bacillus Thuringiensis (Bt) gene, such as in Bt corn. Our inconceivable future will demand much more to be explored in terms of pathogen resistance and weather resistance in crops.

By 2050, advances in genetic modification will allow us to cultivate pest-resistant, drought-tolerant, and nutritionally-enhanced crops that meet the food production demands of our world. Ultimately, it will allow us to produce the most resilient crops the world has ever seen: Heat-resistant crops that mitigate the effects of global warming, drought-tolerant crops that stand up to water shortages, pest-tolerant crops resilient to external harm, and biofortified crops that meet our nutritional needs. With GMOs, our ability to meet our future food and health demands has never looked more optimistic.

CHAPTER 7

CRISPR: THE FRONTIER OF GENE EDITING

———

Maybe GMOs aren't very popular. But CRISPR, the new guy on the gene-editing block, will be. This emerging gene-editing tool will give us the power to quickly and easily create the most resilient and nutritionally-optimal crops the world has ever seen.

I really love bananas. I don't think my life would be complete without them. I religiously freeze them for smoothies, dip them in nut butter as a snack, and use overripe ones to make the most delicious chocolate chip banana bread. It's really the perfect fruit (although plant scientists will tell you it's a herb). With its sweet and soft flesh encased in a peel, bananas are easily transportable, incredibly versatile, and extremely nutritious. With more than 150 countries cultivating over 105 million tonnes of bananas annually, it is easily the most important and popular "fruit" in the world.[1]

When I go back to my home in Malaysia, a bunch of bananas are almost always perched on our fruit bowl. More often than not, the bananas are of the Pisang Awak variety, which is grown at a small farm near my home. Used in banana fritters, the stubby Pisang Awak is the most common variety grown in Malaysia. Back in the U.S., the Cavendish variety dominates. While there are over 1000 varieties of bananas, no other banana is grown or consumed as much as the Cavendish, which accounts for 47% of global banana production.[2] Named after William Cavendish, a British Duke who grew it in his greenhouses at Chatsworth House in the UK, the Cavendish makes up almost the entire banana export market—99% to be exact.[3]

However, the Cavendish wasn't always the most popular banana variety. Before the Cavendish was popularized in the 1950s, the dominant banana variety in Europe and America was the Gros Michel, a thick-skinned, creamier, and sweeter banana.[4] There's a reason it isn't around anymore. By 1965, a strain of fungi called Tropical Race 1 (TR1) had wiped out production of the Gros Michel, forcing major producers to switch to the Cavendish (which is resistant to TR1). Today, just as the Gros Michel was devastated by TR1, the Cavendish is being threatened by a new disease—the Tropical Race 4 (TR4). And out of the 1,000 varieties of bananas, TR4 only affects the Cavendish. Yikes.

Just like TR1, TR4 is deadly. The fungus, which can live undetected in soil for decades, invades banana plants through the roots and then chokes them to death by slowly starving them of water and nutrients. The end result is soil infected by TR4 and a field entirely useless for growing anything.[5]

"When TR4 hits, the destruction is near-total. It looks like somebody's gone to the plantation with a herbicide," explains Randy Ploetz, a professor at the University of Florida's Tropical Research and Education Centre who has spent nearly three decades of his life researching the impacts of TR4.[6]

According to Ploetz, he first learned about TR4 when he received a mysterious package containing infected soil from Taiwan in 1989. Since then, TR4 has spread to Indonesia, Malaysia, Mozambique, Lebanon, Israel, India, Pakistan, Australia, and many more countries. "It's everywhere," urges Ploetz.[7] With fears of TR4 spreading to Latin America, the world's dominant banana producer, Ploetz warns that the Cavendish is at risk of an extinction more catastrophic than the Gros Michel, because unlike the Gros Michel TR1 epidemic, there is no TR4-resistant banana variety to replace the Cavendish. The world is facing a major Cavendish catastrophe.

What is our best chance of saving one of the most important crops in the world without using controversial gene modification techniques? Tropic Biosciences has a solution brewing in its labs. The UK-based biotechnology company is developing TR4-resistant Cavendish bananas using CRISPR, a DNA editing technology shaking the world of genetic crop improvement. The DNA editing molecule called CRISPR-Cas9 is used to molecularly snip off and deactivate specific genes in banana cells. Ultimately, these small tweaks result in banana plants that are resistant to TR4. The company has also used CRISPR to create bananas that ripen more slowly than a normal Cavendish, potentially stopping millions of dollars' worth of bananas from spoiling every year. Evidently, these small genetic tweaks have big implications for a US$12.4 billion banana export market.[8]

The revolutionary thing about using CRISPR is that unlike GMOs, the plant cells that Tropic Biosciences is cultivating is almost genetically identical to any Cavendish banana on the market.[9] Essentially, there is no trace of foreign genes in its banana cells; the slight differences lie in a few genes being switched off. Therefore, CRISPR is arguably not a GM technique. Unlike a highly controversial GM Cavendish banana, a CRISPR-edited, TR4-resistant variety will likely be accepted by consumers worldwide. Ultimately, CRISPR alone could save the Cavendish from extinction.

When *WIRED* writer Matt Reynolds visited Tropic Biosciences' research labs just outside of Norwich, UK, he witnessed the company's CTO, Ofir Meir, "holding the future of the banana in his hand." With rows of grey cell clusters in a Petri dish in hand, Meir confidently exclaimed: "One day, these shoots will become a field in South America."[10]

CHANGING THE BLUEPRINT OF CROPS

So, what exactly is this thing called CRISPR? How does it actually work? CRISPR, which stands for "Clustered Regularly Interspaced Short Palindromic Repeats," is a gene-editing tool derived from the immune systems of bacteria.[11] Co-discovered in 2012 by geneticists Emmanuelle Charpentier and Jennifer Doudna, the CRISPR system is made up of two parts: One part is CRISPR-Cas9, which is the protein that Tropic Biosciences uses to snip or modify DNA strands and is known as the "editing machine."[12] Modified versions of Cas9 also allow researchers to activate gene expression, instead of cutting DNA.[13] The second part of the CRISPR system is the RNA, which guides the Cas9 molecule to the right DNA and serves as the template for encoding a new trait into the plant's DNA.[14]

While there are a few approaches when using CRISPR in plant breeding, a common approach is to insert the CRISPR genes that encode the CRISPR-Cas9 "editing machines" into the plant cell's DNA.[15] When the CRISPR-Cas9 gene is active, it approaches specific genes in the DNA and modifies them by deleting or inserting anything from a single base pair to a large gene. In some cases, it also rewrites the relevant sections of the plant genome to help a new trait to manifest. From correcting genetic errors in humans to preventing diseases to creating new genetic variations of crops, the use cases of CRISPR are incredibly diverse.

A good example of how CRISPR can be used is in "dwarfing" tall crops for easier harvesting. To make a tall plant shorter, you need to reduce gibberellin—the "plant height hormone." The amount of gibberellin being produced is controlled by the GA20-ox gene.[16] So if we wanted to create a variety of short palm trees using CRISPR, we would first insert the CRISPR genes that encode the CRISPR-Cas9 "editing machines" into the palm plant's DNA. When the CRISPR-Cas9 gene is active, it can efficiently locate specific DNA sequences that create the GA20-ox gene. By rewriting relevant DNA sequences, CRISPR-Cas9 can reduce the production of GA20-ox and therefore lower the amount of gibberellin being released. As a result, reduced gibberellin causes the palm oil tree to grow shorter, making it easier to harvest. Remember that tissue culture lab near my home in Malaysia? Shorter palm trees are exactly the desired outcomes of that lab. However, instead of using conventional breeding techniques, using CRISPR can achieve this outcome much faster, cheaper, and easier.

In the last few years, CRISPR has received major attention. It has gone so far as to be called "the biggest biotech discovery of the century."[17] The largest CRISPR biotech company, CRISPR Therapeutics, had an initial public offering (IPO) in 2016, just three years after it was founded. Impressively, CRISPR Therapeautics' share price was up 44% within less than a year on the public markets.[18] Clearly, CRISPR has managed to incite significant optimism for the future of gene editing.

Hope or hype, why is CRISPR such a flaming hot topic? Essentially, it is the most simple, versatile, and precise gene-editing method that has successfully worked in the history of humankind. With CRISPR, editing genes has become quicker than other gene engineering techniques; it achieves desired outcomes in days rather than weeks or months. We're talking about a powerful new genetic tool that can control exactly which genes get expressed in plants, animals, and even humans. We're talking about the ability to delete undesirable traits and potentially add desirable traits with more precision than ever before.[19]

While plant scientists have traditionally looked to conventional plant breeding to edit the crop genome, this method can only take us so far—within a species or very closely related species. Conventional plant breeding is relatively inefficient, with unpredictable outcomes and long periods of testing to develop reliable strains. On the other hand, GMOs are incredibly effective in achieving genetic crop improvements, but its widespread adoption is undeniably controversial. Admittedly, the lack of acceptance of GMOs is still a barrier to overcome. However, CRISPR, dubbed "the biggest science story of the decade", offers an excellent solution for the future of agriculture.[20]

ARE CRISPR CROPS CONSIDERED GMOS?

The biggest question facing the success of CRISPR today is whether CRISPR crops can be called GMOs. Simply put, the consideration of CRISPR as a non-GM technique is critical to its major adoption in agriculture. As defined in Chapter 6, the most common definition of GMOs is from the Codex Alimentarius, which states that GMOs are "any living organism that possesses a novel combination of genetic material obtained through the use of modern biotechnology."[21] Applying this to CRISPR, most CRISPR crops do not possess "a novel combination of genetic material." Without a trace of foreign genes, the genome of a CRISPR-edited Cavendish is almost identical to any other Cavendish banana on the market. And without containing foreign genetic material, CRISPR crops simply cannot be deemed GMOs.

CRISPR-edited crops that leave no trace of foreign DNA have already been successfully created. In April 2016, Yinong Yang, a plant pathologist at Pennsylvania State University, used CRISPR to engineer the white button mushroom to resist browning.[22] The final button mushroom product showed no trace of the CRISPR-Cas9 gene or any antibiotic markers used in the process; it was the same white button mushroom, with a small deletion of the enzyme responsible for browning. Therefore, it is fair to assume that using CRISPR in gene editing doesn't leave traces of foreign material, with the modified host being almost identical, if not bio-similar, to the original plant. Ultimately, this was enough to convince the

United States Department of Agricultural (USDA) to approve of the CRISPR-edited, non-browning mushroom.[23]

While CRISPR companies and researchers market CRISPR-edited crops as non-GMO, critics argue that they should be considered GMO. The argument is that CRISPR still involves the genetic alteration of a plant by inserting the CRISPR-Cas9 molecule (considered by some to be foreign genetic material). However, this argument is hardly convincing. By the time a crop completes its life cycle from germination to the production of seeds, the CRISPR-Cas9 molecule would be eliminated from the edited crop. The seeds these plants produce do not actually carry the CRISPR genes; they simply inherit the new traits. On the other hand, traditional GMOs have foreign DNA inserted into its genome in order for the crop to take on a new trait.

If all this isn't convincing enough for CRISPR critics, scientists have gone even further to ensure CRISPR can be considered a non-GMO; they've successfully developed gene-edited plants *without* introducing the "foreign" CRISPR gene. In May 2018, plant geneticists at the University of Connecticut, in conjunction with Nanjing Agricultural University, Jiangsu Academy of Agricultural Sciences, University of Florida, Hunan Agricultural University, and the University of California San Diego, developed a technique that uses CRISPR to create desirable characteristics in crops without the direct introduction of foreign bacterial genes.[24] Very simply, their technique involves taking plant cells and mixing them with a CRISPR-engineered soil microbe. The mixture is then left to incubate for a few days, giving the soil microbe time to "infect" the plant cells and deliver the gene-editing machinery, which then alters the plant's genetic code.[25] This method prevents CRISPR genes from becoming part of the plant's genome and merely causes the plant to do the work of gene editing.

It's safe to say that CRISPR crops don't contain foreign genes, nor does it require the insertion of foreign material to introduce CRISPR into target cells. Even if a bacterium is used to introduce CRISPR, it actually leaves behind no trace. The plant genome being modified is almost identical to the original; the USDA approved, non-browning mushroom was genetically the same mushroom, just without the browning enzyme.

So, can CRISPR crops be considered GMOs? CRISPR genetically modifies a crop's genome, but it doesn't necessarily result in a genetically modified organism. The key for CRISPR's success moving forward, is for the scientific community, governments, and consumers to understand this critical distinction. Once they do, CRISPR can be widely accepted as a non-GM technique.

UNLOCKING THE UNTAPPED
BIODIVERSITY OF CROPS

Dr. Joyce Van Eck has been intrigued by genetic crop improvement ever since her undergraduate days at Pennsylvania State

University. A plant breeder and geneticist by training, she is currently the director of the Center for Plant Biotechnology Research at the Boyce Thompson Institute (BTI) in Ithaca, New York and a faculty member at Cornell University.[26] When I first spoke to Van Eck, her passion for her lab's focus on biotechnological approaches to crop improvement was infectious. She spoke excitedly about BTI's recent work in using CRISPR to breed ground cherries. You see, the ground cherry project all started with Van Eck and her lab's research into tomatoes, the "white mice of plant research." Like many research labs, Van Eck's lab used a reversed genetics approach to identify genes that correspond to specific traits. Once Van Eck had learned a lot about tomatoes, she soon became wildly interested in using her findings to fast track crop domestication and improvement in other crops.[27]

"A key trait for domestication is making unmanageable growth more manageable so that it can be used for agricultural production, for instance, more fruit or bigger sized fruits, " she explains.[28]

Her lab's next project would be to leverage the knowledge on tomatoes and apply it to a crop distantly related to the tomato. She soon came across the ground cherry. Concealed in a light green husk, the ground cherry resembles a cherry tomato, but is much sweeter and fruitier. Packed with nutrients and full of anti-inflammatory and medicinal properties, the ground cherry has largely remained in the wild and has had little done to improve or domesticate it.

Due to its sprawling weedy growth, measly fruit, and high fruit drop rates, wild ground cherries are largely unsuitable for commercial agriculture.[29]

Van Eck's lab changed all that. They used CRISPR to alter specific ground cherry genes that affected specific characteristics. The result? Ground cherry plants with larger fruit (50% more fruit on a stem compared to the wild variety!) and compact fruit clusters that made harvesting easier.[30] The lab also managed to use CRISPR to greatly reduce fruit drop, reducing the risk of damage and alleviating food safety concerns for the ground cherry. In the future, Van Eck hopes that the ground cherry can be cultivated and marketed as the next superfood berry. Packed with essential vitamins and blessed with several beneficial properties, ground cherries are nutritional and functional powerhouses. They could even be the next blueberry. Needless to say, I told Van Eck that I'd absolutely love to try one.

Domesticating more crops like the ground cherry is really important in a world where the biodiversity of crop cultivation is severely limited. Of the 250,000 plant species known to humans, only 7,000 species (2.8%) have been consumed and 120 species have been cultivated.[31] Furthermore, only 15 crops provide 90% of the world's food energy intake, with just three crops—rice, wheat, and maize—making up two thirds of this.[32] Can you see how this is deeply concerning? Mostly due to the lack of crop domestication, we cultivate only a small portion of what is available to us in nature.

That's like going to a buffet and only eating from the dessert section (though I won't judge you if you do).

Perhaps one of the biggest lessons in the importance of genetic biodiversity is the near devastation of rice fields in the 1970s.[33] During this time, a deadly grassy stunt virus was infesting rice fields across Asia, endangering one of the world's most important food crops. Thankfully, a gene from a distant Indian wild rice variety was used to confer resistance in the dominant rice variety, essentially saving it from extinction. Today, that dominant rice variety is grown across 11 million hectares of Asian rice fields.[34] Without that virus-resistant gene from the Indian wild rice variety, the white rice that we grow and consume today wouldn't exist. What the history of rice in the 1970s teaches us is that in order to withstand environmental and disease threats like the grassy stunt virus, we must make crop biodiversity a priority. Because when we do, we increase the genetic base of our crops—the basic database of genes that can provide crucial resistance or immunity for other crop species.

The lack of biodiversity in agriculture today can be largely attributed to monoculture farming. Monoculture farming, the cultivation of only a single crop in a specified area, has become as ubiquitous in agriculture as the iPhone is in the mobile phone world. But while the consistency and uniformity of monoculture farming optimizes one crop's production, it threatens the health and balance of the entire agricultural system. Because when you intensely grow one crop, the reliance on that one crop is almost too massive to be smart. Just like investors aim to invest in a diverse portfolio to mitigate risks and optimize returns, it's smarter for farmers to grow a diverse array of crops to safeguard the world's sustenance.

One of the most infamous examples of the dangers of relying on one crop variety is of the Irish Potato Famine in the 1840s.[35] At the time, Irish farmers grew a single variety of potato. In 1845, the potato late blight fungus soon spread rapidly throughout Ireland, destroying nearly half the potato crop that year and about three-quarters of all potato crops over the next seven years.[36] Just like potato fields during the Great Irish Potato Famine, monoculture fields today risk mass infestation. Compared to a field filled with a diverse array of crop species, monocultures are much more susceptible to pests spreading quickly with little resistance.

In the pursuance of highly-uniform monocultures, we've ended up severely limiting crop biodiversity. This loss of genetic diversity ultimately leads to limited knowledge regarding varieties and the lack of genetic material available for use in plant improvement. And as the Irish Potato Famine demonstrates, a lack of crop diversity also makes farmers much more vulnerable to external harms like pests and diseases.

The promotion of genetic biodiversity is critically important in our current world of commercial, monoculture-centric agriculture. The genes found in the largely untapped pool of undomesticated crops can provide a wealth of crop improvement opportunities that we will need to feed our world well. And just like Joyce Van Eck was able to use CRISPR to domesticate the ground cherry, the continued development of CRISPR-edited crops will accelerate the domestication of more wild crops. With CRISPR, we can bring a greater variety of crop varieties to market and hugely improve the earth's crop biodiversity.

UNCERTAIN REGULATORY PATHWAY FOR CRISPR

So how have regulators approached CRISPR-edited crops so far? There have been mixed reactions. On the bright side, the USDA has mostly welcomed CRISPR-edited crops, stating in March 2018 that it would *not* regulate nor oversee "a set of new techniques that are increasingly being used by plant breeders to produce new plant varieties that are indistinguishable from those developed through traditional breeding methods."[37] Basically, only if CRISPR crops contained foreign genetic material would they trigger the USDA to re-classify them as a GMO. The way the USDA sees it, using gene editing to make a small genetic tweak is something so minuscule that it could happen in the process of natural selection anyway. In other words, U.S. regulators see CRISPR as a technique to accelerate the plant breeding process. To them, a CRISPR-edited mushroom is just a mushroom.

The USDA's classification of CRISPR engineered crops and seeds as non-GMO ultimately breaks down regulatory barriers for CRISPR to take off. However, anti-GMO organizations like The Non-GMO project have vilified this lack of oversight, arguing that any alteration to DNA is considered genetic modification of organisms.[38] By that definition, however, even selective and conventional breeding techniques that have been used for centuries would be considered GMOs.

Unlike the U.S., the EU has a very different approach. In July 2018, the European Court of Justice ruled that new genetic engineering techniques like CRISPR would still be considered GMOs and are subject to the EU's GMO Directive.[39] This was decided on the basis that gene-editing techniques that alter the genetic material of an organism in an unnatural way are still considered GMOs, unless it is a conventional and food safety proven method. While this is currently discouraging for CRISPR, rapid advancements in CRISPR-edited crops will soon convince EU regulators that a CRISPR crop is virtually bio-identical to the original crop, with small insertions, deletions, or alterations of the crop's original genome. For the hundredth time, there is no trace of foreign genetic material in a CRISPR crop.

At the end of the day, policymakers in the U.S. and the EU prioritize food safety and are merely concerned with the contamination of foreign genetic material in the end product. The final product, and whether it is "substantially different" to the non-modified version, will be a key factor in the regulation of CRISPR. And while the EU has indirectly classified CRISPR as a GMO, it is hard to say if the rest of the world will follow suit. Considering there has yet to be any substantial studies showing the effects of CRISPR crops on human health, more research to prove it is safe will need to be done to convince regulators. Once research has been done to prove it is safe and people truly understand what CRISPR crops are, my bets are that they will not vilify it, but embrace it as a gene-editing tool necessary for our anti-GMO world.

THE FRONTIER OF GENE EDITING

Whether in agriculture or medicine, CRISPR is the most groundbreaking biotechnology discovery of the century. The truth is, traditional methods of plant breeding take years of research with uncertain outcomes. On the other hand, CRISPR techniques are faster, more efficient, and more accurate than any gene-editing technology ever discovered.

Without leaving behind a trace of foreign DNA, CRISPR is helping us create the crops of the future. It'll domesticate wild crops to increase our earth's biodiversity. It'll accelerate the development of better crops that tolerate external environmental threats. It'll create crops that require less inputs like water. And it'll enhance the functional and nutritional quality of our crops, boosting the health of the most hunger-stricken people in developing nations.

CRISPR co-inventor Jennifer Doudna envisions the future of CRISPR:

"Within the next few years, this new biotechnology will give us higher-yielding crops, healthier livestock, and more nutritious foods... We are on the cusp of a new era in the history of life on earth—an age in which humans exercise an unprecedented level of control over the genetic composition of the species that co-inhabit our planet."[40]

With CRISPR, the possibilities are endless; we can change genetic behavior, turn on or off genes, and create entirely new traits. This frontier in gene editing will bring about a world where genetic tinkering will be easier, safer, and cheaper. In a resource-constraint and highly uncertain future, it will entirely revolutionize how we feed the world.

CHAPTER 8

A BETTER WAY TO (M)EAT

———

Food scientists are reinventing the way we (m)eat. By 2050, we will no longer need to feed, breed, and slaughter animals for protein. By 2050, we will eat meat that is either clean or plant-based, much better for our health and the environment, and just as delicious.

It's 2030, and you're shopping at a grocery store in preparation for Sunday's Barbecue; burgers are definitely on the menu. So, you walk towards the beef section and see racks of packaged ground beef patties. You see three different products: the supermarket's private label 80/20 ground beef patties, Memphis Meats' 100% clean ground beef patties, and Beyond Meat's plant-based burger patties.

To be honest, they all look the same. But while the 80/20 ground beef and Memphis Meats' 100% clean ground beef patties are the same price—US$3.99 per pound—, the Beyond Meat burger patties are slightly cheaper per pound. You normally buy the 80/20 ground beef patties for burgers, but pick up the Memphis Meats clean ground beef out of curiosity. You read:

"No Antibiotics. No Bacterial Contamination. No Animal Suffering. Our beef uses 99% less land, 96% less water, and produces 96% less greenhouse gas emissions compared to conventional ground beef."[1]

What kind of choice will you make?

This is the future of meat. This is the future of your burgers, your meatballs, and your chicken tenders. Let me tell you why.

THE CLEAN MEAT REVOLUTION

Animals are horribly inefficient vehicles for producing meat. A mere look at the feed conversion ratios (the mass of feed needed to produce the same mass of meat) of animals we consume show that there are great inefficiencies in the ability of livestock and poultry to convert feed into meat. A chicken, the most efficient land animal, requires 4.5 kg of feed to create 1 kg of chicken meat.[2] Pigs need 9.4 kg of feed to create 1 kg of pork. Cows need 25 kg of feed to create 1 kg of beef.[3] Clean meat requires no feed to create 1 kg of meat.

But what exactly is clean meat? Clean meat, or cell-cultured meat, is essentially real meat produced from animal cells without animal slaughter. Commonly known as lab-grown meat, it is made by extracting animal muscle tissue cultures, adding a growth medium (the nutrient bath fed to cells to help them grow and replicate) and putting the tissue cultures in a suitable environment to self-replicate and grow.[4] The tissues grow more muscle that can be harvested within a few weeks and can then be formed into meatballs, burger patties, chicken strips, or other meat products.

This groundbreaking, emerging technology bypasses the need to rear animals altogether and removes the element of an animal out of the meat equation. And because a living animal is not involved, the production of clean meat is aseptic, with little to no risk of bacteria or fungi growth. Clean meat will literally be "clean" and free from antibiotics, fecal matter, pathogens, and other contaminants found in conventional meat. With clean meat, we can say goodbye to animal-related E.Coli or Salmonella outbreaks.

Apart from the greatly inefficient feed conversion ratios of animals, the incredible amount of other resources consumed by animal agriculture is alarming for the future of our planet. In one of the most comprehensive studies published in the journal *Science*, it was found that by eradicating consumption of meat and dairy produced in our current systems, global farmland use could be reduced by more than 75%—an area equivalent to the U.S., China, European Union, and

Australia combined—and *still* feed the world.[5] The analysis also revealed that while meat and dairy provides just 18% of calories and 37% of our protein intake, it uses the vast majority—namely 83%—of farmland and produces 60% of agriculture's greenhouse gas emissions.[6] Those are some shocking numbers. The intense amounts of farmland used and pollutants created by meat and dairy easily makes it the world's two most resource-intensive and polluting industries.

If that wasn't shocking enough, I've got more news for you; meat production uses up more than a quarter of the world's water footprint.[7] In comparison, water use at home only uses 4% of the world's water footprint. That means changing your diet could have a bigger impact on reducing your water footprint than using less water to shower, cook, and clean at home. Even crazier, is that it takes 4,219% more water to produce a pound of beef than it does a pound of pulses.[8] Needless to say, meat and dairy consumption is not only significantly contributing to global warming, it is also putting immense strain on our world's freshwater resources. Considering that by 2050, more than 50% of the world's population will face some form of water stress or scarcity, a different way of producing meat is desperately needed.[9]

The fact of the matter is that our current industrial animal agricultural system is not working for the health of humans nor for the health of our planet. The arrival of clean meat is going to forever change meat production as we know it. Essentially, we've discovered a way to grow meat in the *same* way that animals do, but without having to rear an animal that both damages the environment and consumes a vast amount of the world's key resources.

Considering its wide-ranging impacts, the clean meat industry hasn't gone without notice. Clean meat technology companies have garnered widespread interest amongst the business and venture capital (VC) world, with major corporations and investors flocking to invest in these companies. Memphis Meats, a pioneer of clean meat, received over US$20 million in funding from large corporations like Tyson Foods and Cargill and big name investors like Bill Gates and Richard Branson.[10] JUST, another company working on clean meat amongst other sustainable animal products, has a whopping US$220 million in funding from prominent investors like Khosla Ventures, Horizons Ventures and again, Bill Gates.[11] Evidently, the entire business community is seeing the US$928 billion global meat industry as an area hungry for investment.[12] In the business world, this usually translates to an industry that is ripe for disruption.

The business and VC community are not the only ones supporting clean meat. Shockingly, clean meat is also garnering major support from animal rights groups. You heard that right—animal rights groups. In fact, People for the Ethical Treatment of Animals (PETA), the most prominent animal rights group of all, actually praised the technology for its potential to "save billions of animals per year, improve the environment, and reinvent big agriculture as we know it."[13] With this groundbreaking method of producing real meat, science has made cruelty-free real meat a reality—even vegans and animal rights activists would eat it!

Clearly, clean meat will forever change meat production as we know it. Not only is clean meat safeguarding animal welfare, it is providing a viable solution to the sustainability and human health issues of traditional meat production. The fact that two of the biggest meat producers in the world, Cargill and Tyson, have invested in clean meat technology, signals that replacing conventional meat with "cleaner" meat is truly the future of animal protein. As they say, if you can't beat them, join them.

DEMYSTIFYING THE CLEAN MEAT PERCEPTION

In a bustling atrium at Cornell University, Aylon Steinhart speaks, in a way only a vegan could, with a deep passion for plant-based and cell-cultured meat. Growing up on a farm in Israel, Aylon developed an interest in business and the environment ever since he was a little boy. When he was just seven years old, he went door-to-door in his small town of Kohav Ya'ir collecting donations for Israel's nature protection fund.[14] At the Good Food Institute (GFI), one of the leading organizations working with scientists, investors, and entrepreneurs in the clean meat and plant-based protein industry, Aylon was a Business Innovation Specialist working with entrepreneurs to launch the next generation of innovative food startups.

Considering my obsession with the sustainable meat movement, my interview with Aylon is probably one of the most eye-opening interviews I have done for this book. Needless to say, I had to ask him what he thought about the stigma associated with meat grown in a lab.

He had a firm response:

"The future of clean meat is essentially in a bioreactor or brewery. It's gonna look like something that's familiar, not in Petri dishes or labs, essentially what beer production is, in these big bioreactors where the meat is grown or "brewed" and then harvested. And yeah, these products are now produced in a lab, but in the future they are going to be produced like any other product. For example, we don't think of Budweiser as starting off in a lab, but Budweiser too started in a lab. The perception of clean meat as "lab grown" will lessen and lessen as the product becomes more standardized in its production and when people get more exposed to it through education."[15]

Changing our perception of meat production is one of the biggest barriers to clean meat acceptance. When you tell someone that clean meat is currently grown in a lab instead of a live animal, they immediately squirm and conjure up images of meat cells in Petri dishes. While it is true that clean meat involves testing in Petri dishes and labs at the early stages, like Aylon says, the future of clean meat production will involve producing meat at scale in bioreactors—similar to beer production.[16]

Bruce Friedrich, executive director of GFI has the same vision for the future of meat: "Growing meat at scale will look more like a beer brewery or a greenhouse, not like a laboratory."[17]

It's hard to believe that growing meat in a brewery is the future; after all, the only images of meat production we've known are of animals roaming on a farm and of industrial factory farms and slaughterhouses—the end game for animals. However, the discomfort we feel when learning about cell-cultured meat grown in a lab is no more substantiated than knowing that processed foods like cereal and Cheetos started off in a food lab. The difference, according to Friedrich, is that "unlike processed food, the final product (meat) is the same as the original product produced in nature."[18] That's a pretty wild revelation in a food world where virtually everything is extensively processed and loaded with additives (even the "100%" ground beef you buy likely contains pink slime, an additive used to reduce the overall fat content of ground beef).[19]

Apart from the indistinguishable nature of clean meat and conventional meat, the contrasting images of industrial animal agriculture and clean meat production is enough to eliminate any negative perceptions of clean meat. In industrial animal production, slaughterhouses are gruesome, dirty, and wildly secretive with special laws preventing cameras from even being installed. Now imagine a clean meat facility that is 100% sterile with glass walls that give you a transparent view of production. Wouldn't you feel better knowing that clean meat is produced in a facility that is much cleaner than industrial slaughterhouses? Ultimately, the clean meat industry has nothing to hide. That's far from what I can say about the industrial meat industry.

Consumer skepticism of cell-cultured meat is understandable, but interestingly enough, consumer demand seems to be there; a 2017 study conducted by the University of Queensland, Australia, found that 70.6% of consumers in the U.S. are interested in trying lab grown beef.[20] The study also found that one third of Americans would be willing to eat clean meat regularly or as a replacement for farmed meat. While this may come as a shock to others, I am not surprised. When it comes down to it, consumers are driven by taste, price, and convenience. If clean meat looks and tastes the same as conventional meat, is just as affordable, and is readily available on our supermarket aisles, then what's stopping consumers from purchasing it? Far from deterring consumers, the novelty of clean meat technology may even intrigue consumers enough for them to try it.

"Eventually cultured meat will be cheaper and more sustainable. And we'll have so many people on the planet that there just won't be another option. The human race is progressing, technology is progressing, and eventually, people are going to get used to this idea," says Shier Friedman, co-founder of Modern Agriculture Foundation, a pro-cultured meat company trying to grow entire chicken breasts.[21] Yes, complex, three-dimensional organs. Don't cringe—it's the future of your meat!

If we want to nourish the world sustainably in the future, we'll have no choice but to find innovative ways of producing our meat. And since clean meat is identical to conventional meat, it will eventually be embraced by consumers who can feel ethically and environmentally good about their choice of protein.

CLEAN MEAT ECONOMICS

Clean meat sounds great on paper, but why hasn't it been brought to market? An immense hurdle to clean meat commercialization is the overwhelming costs of producing the meat. The world's first lab grown burger, produced in 2013 by Maastricht University researcher Mark Post, costs US$330,000 to produce.[22] Considering it requires fewer inputs like water and land, clean meat should theoretically be cheaper than conventional meat. Still that is not the case. Like many commercial products, the cost per pound reductions in clean meat will require taking the technology that works at a small scale (in a lab) and making it large scale (in a bioreactor).

Liz Specht, PhD, senior scientist at the Good Food Institute (GFI), says that amongst all the unique challenges in clean meat production, "the biggest challenge is the bioreactor scale up, although every stage has unique challenges."[23]

As mentioned, bioreactors are the containers used to facilitate the biological reactions required in clean meat production.

In these bioreactors, all clean meat starts out as tissue culture cells. An important aspect of clean meat production is the ability to work with cells that can differentiate into all cell types (muscle, fat, connective tissue). Especially for high-end cuts of meat like steak, these cell lines require bio-based 'scaffolding', which provides structure for the cells to attach to and grow.[24] A component of the bioreactor, the scaffolding structure also directs the differentiation of cell types, ensuring that cells grow in a way that replicates the taste, texture, and appearance of conventionally produced meat. At this stage, the right ratio of fat, muscle, and connective tissue must also be achieved. As you can tell, producing clean meat at scale is quite a complicated undertaking. Currently, these types of bioreactors do not exist at the scale required for mass production of clean meat.

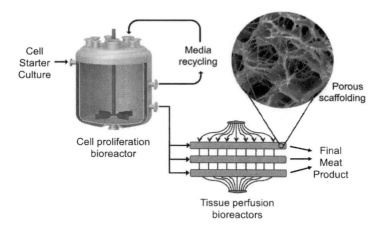

This illustrates an example of the clean meat production process at scale.

Source: The Good Food Institute (GFI)

While scaling is a challenge, another challenge is overcoming the high costs of production inputs. Theoretically, fewer inputs are needed in clean meat than in conventional meat, but even at scale, the costs of these inputs are extremely high. Amongst the largest input costs is the growth media that feeds the animal tissue cells. Growth media, the nutrient bath that cells need to survive and grow, contains amino acids, sugars, vitamins, and growth factors. Ten to twenty percent of the growth media is composed of growth factors derived from animal serum—a blend of growth-inducing proteins typically made from foetal blood.[25]

There are two major issues with these growth factors. Firstly, the use of animal serum, especially foetal bovine serum (FBS), is hugely controversial from an ethical point of view. Hence, several companies like JUST and cell-cultured fish startup Finless Foods have been searching for ways to produce growth factors derived from plant-based sources. Considering the significant developments in biotechnology, the future could also open up possibilities to artificially produce growth factors using recombinant DNA technology. Mark Post, co-founder of Mosa Meat and creator of the world's first cultured burger, has already tested cells in 400 different conditions to see how they respond to different growth factors and conditions. "It's a matter of time. It's just going through the alternatives that there are and optimizing them," he says.[26]

Another issue is that animal serum is incredibly costly. A single liter of FBS costs between US$398 and US$928, and the clean meat industry is going through buckets of this miracle juice every day.[27] Mark Post, co-founder of Mosa Meat and creator of the world's first cell-cultured burger, estimates that it takes 50 liters of serum to produce a single beef burger patty. Clearly, we're still a long way off the price level needed to make clean meat a realistic alternative to conventional meat.

A big part of why these growth factors are extremely expensive is because those currently used in clean meat are biotech-grade growth factors used in pharmaceuticals. These growth factors are usually produced in small volumes, where only tiny amounts are needed to grow cell clusters for biomedical research.[28] On the other hand, the clean meat industry will need to grow cells at a significantly larger scale. The hope is that growing demand for growth factors from the clean meat industry will incite the biotech industry to produce serum at scale, bringing down its sky-high cost.

In the future, I think we'll see biotech companies specifically producing growth factors for use in commercial cell-cultured meat production. Aylon Steinhart from GFI has a similar belief. He says that "by scaling back growth factor quality and finding ways to use more cost-efficient, food grade quality growth factors, we can bring the costs of clean meat down to be comparable to conventional meat production."[29] Like Mark Post said, it's just a matter of time.

While clean meat isn't yet cheap enough to be produced commercially, production costs are seriously plummeting. In the fall of 2016, Memphis Meats unveiled the world's first cell-cultured meatball.[30] At the time, it cost Memphis Meats US\$18,000 per pound (US\$8,165 per kg) to produce, but in less than two years, the company managed to drive costs down by 87% at US\$2,400 per pound (US\$1,089 per kg).[31] Following this rate of cost reduction, Dr. Uma Valeti, Memphis Meats' CEO, predicts the company will be able to have its products in supermarkets by 2021 and mass produce clean meat at prices equal to, or below, that of conventional meat.[32] Paul Shapiro, author of *Clean Meat: How Growing Meat Without Animals Will Revolutionize Dinner and the World*, also believes that we will see clean meat on shelves by 2021.[33]

Despite Valeti's and Shapiro's estimates, 2021 is remarkably optimistic. Beyond cost barriers, there are still regulatory and consumer perception hurdles facing cell cultured meat acceptance. Lengthy regulatory approval processes coupled by the time required to develop suitable equipment and production processes at scale will defer clean meat commercialization. Realistically, it will be at least 10 to 15 years before clean meat is commercially viable or even competitively close to the price of conventional meat. So, don't be surprised if 10 to 15 years from now, you see 100% clean meat at your regular grocery store!

AN OPTIMISTIC REGULATORY
PATH FOR CLEAN MEAT

In October 2018, the U.S. Food and Drug Administration (FDA) and the U.S. Department of Agriculture (USDA) held the world's first ever joint meeting about regulation on cell-cultured meat.[34] While a conclusion as to whether cell cultured meat can be considered meat has not been reached, the FDA and USDA confirmed that they would jointly regulate clean meat: the FDA will conduct pre-market product approval and the USDA will oversee cell-cultured meat products once it is commercially available on the market.[35]

In a statement, the FDA said that "given information we have at the time, it seems reasonable to think that cultured meat, if manufactured in accordance with appropriate safety standards and all relevant regulations, could be consumed safely."[36] The involvement of the USDA, whose jurisdiction has always lied in meat, poultry, and egg products, is significant for the future of clean meat; it's a strong signal that clean meat will eventually be classified as meat and be regulated as tightly as conventional meat producers. What's even more encouraging, is that this atypical "hybrid approach" in which the FDA and USDA have chosen to work together is a strong indicator that food and agricultural policy makers are prioritizing clean meat commercialization. Clearly, policy makers are waking up to the significant environmental and human health benefits that clean meat brings.

While regulatory acceptance still lies in murky waters, labeling is another issue. What should we call clean meat? Will regulators give it a special label like "cell-cultured meat" that differentiates it from conventionally produced meat? Can the product be labeled according to the animal it came from—say, "pork" or "chicken?"

One thing is for sure, we should not be calling it "lab-grown meat." Considering the future of cell-cultured meat production, that's a deceiving term. It just grosses people out. Every time I even mentioned "lab-grown meat" to people, they immediately squirm with deep discomfort. Realistically, terms like "lab-grown meat" and "cell-cultured meat" are not particularly consumer friendly, so the Good Food Institute (GFI) has encouraged people to use the term 'clean meat.'

"The phrase 'clean meat' is similar to 'clean energy' in that it communicates important aspects of the technology—both the environmental benefits and the decrease in food-borne pathogens and drug residues." GFI's executive director Bruce Friedrich argues.[37]

However, the term "clean meat" has understandably received backlash from traditional animal farmers, who take offense with the implication that conventionally produced meat is "dirty." Even labeling cell cultured meat as "meat" has been a significant topic of debate; the U.S. Cattle Association has long opposed labeling cell-cultured meat as "meat."[38] But considering the USDA's involvement, a likely outcome is that regulators will mandate that meat be labeled meat, regardless of whether it is produced in-vitro (outside the animal) or in-vivo (inside the animal).

While the U.S. has made great regulatory strides and shown its openness to clean meat, clean mean regulation is still a novelty for major governments around the world. As the commercialization of clean meat soon reaches places beyond the US, regulators around the world will need to decide how to regulate clean meat in comparison to conventional meat. And since clean meat is essentially real meat, other governments may actually choose not to regulate it or be more lax on regulation. With great delays and remaining uncertainty in clean meat's regulatory landscape in the U.S., clean meat companies like JUST have actually considered launching their products in countries with looser regulations, like China or Singapore.[39]

At the end of the day, clean meat is real food and in fact, real meat. It is not a new drug, or an additive, nor a supplement. As long as companies and regulators are on the same page regarding how these products will meet food safety standards, clean meat should be able to enter any global market successfully with little regulatory barriers.

Despite the potential of clean meat to revolutionize animal protein, we will only start seeing clean meat on supermarket shelves as early as 2030. While clean meat has garnered significant initial hype, another meat alternative has arguably gotten even more attention as it makes its way into mainstream consumer markets.

PLANT-BASED MEAT POWER

When the Beyond Burger launched in 2016 at Whole Foods Market in Boulder, Colorado, it was the first vegan burger patty ever to be sold alongside conventional meat products. Believe it or not, it sold out in under an hour.[40] Since then, Beyond Meat, the company producing these plant-based burgers, has seen its flagship Beyond Burger outsell traditional beef at major supermarkets.

According to Ethan Brown, founder and CEO of Beyond Meat, "in Southern California—in one of the largest conventional retailers in the country—we are now the number one selling patty in the meat case."[41] And true enough, in April 2018, Beyond Meat really did sell more vegan "beef" than Angus beef patties, 80/20 beef, and even grass-fed beef patties by unit. What is even crazier about all this is that the Beyond Burger is more expensive than conventional beef. It costs US$5.99 for two four-ounce patties—almost twice the price of conventional beef per ounce.[42] That's wild. It is the antithesis of everything I learned about supply and demand; demand for a product simply doesn't increase relative to other goods that are lower in price. The popularity of the Beyond Burger really is a testament to the growing appetite for plant-based meat that actually tastes good. It's a signal that the doors are wide open for disruption of the US$928 billion global meat industry.[43]

In the past, plant-based or "mock" meats have largely been confined to the province of vegetarians and vegans, who flock to the "vegetarian" and "frozen vegetarian" aisles of the grocery store in search of a meat substitute. As demand for the Beyond Burger has shown, that notion is drastically changing with the rise of plant-based meat—plant-derived products that accurately mimic the taste, texture, and look of real meat. Valued at US$4.6 billion in 2018, the global market for meat alternatives is set to reach US$6.3 billion by 2023.[44]

While the Beyond Burger has attracted a lot of attention, the entire plant-based meat industry has experienced similar hikes in sales growth. Since early 2017, there has been a massive boom in demand for plant-based meat products. Within a year to June 2018, U.S. retail sales of plant-based meats were up 24%, outpacing the overall food industry sales growth of just 2% in the same period.[45] The numbers don't lie—plant-based meat is a booming industry stomping its way into the mainstream.

The interesting thing about the plant-based meat space is that it isn't new. Companies like UK-based Quorn and U.S.-based LightLife have been making plant-based foods for decades. However, when plant-based meat first entered the scene, it was generally geared towards vegetarians. The meat substitutes of the past were highly processed, specifically marketed as substitutes, and generally tasted like cardboard. But today, a new wave of plant-based meat innovation is completely changing the meat alternative game. You see, plant-based meat companies today don't see their customers as vegetarians, they see them as meat eaters. Beyond Meat, the company which outsold conventional beef, refuses to sell in a store unless its products are placed in the meat section. Why? Because they want to be indistinguishable to meat. The crazy thing is, these plant-based meats actually taste like meat.

In 2013, Bill Gates, a keen investor of both plant-based and clean meat, tried a chicken taco made with Beyond Meat's plant-based chicken meat. His experience is enough to convince you:

"Like most people, I don't think I can be easily fooled. But that's just what happened when I was asked to taste a chicken taco and tell whether the meat inside was real or fake.

The meat certainly had the look and the smell of chicken. I took a bite and it had the taste and texture of real chicken, too. But I was surprised to learn that there wasn't an ounce of real chicken it. The 'meat' was made entirely of plants. And yet, I couldn't tell the difference.

What I was experiencing was more than a clever meat substitute. It was a taste of the future of food."[46]

If Bill Gates tells you that the plant-based chicken in his taco tastes like real meat, you'd better believe him.

With its products so closely resembling conventional meat, the plant-based meat industry will continue to wow people like Bill Gates with its vegan "meat." And in the coming years, the overwhelming demand for meat alternatives will see products like the Beyond Burger aggressively chip away at traditional meat market share. Already, plant-based meat companies are growing like crazy. Beyond Meat is currently in more than 25,000 restaurants and grocery stores across the U.S., including Wal-Mart, Target, and T.G.I Friday's. Since launching in 2016, the company has sold more than 25 million burger patties and is actively expanding globally, rolling out in 50 countries including in the UK.[47]

Impossible Foods, another major plant-based meat player, leverages plant-derived heme, an iron-rich molecule usually found in animal protein, to create "bleeding" burger patties that replicate the meaty flavor of conventional beef. With more than US$500 million in venture funding, Impossible Foods has become one of the most highly funded food technology companies of all time and is available in more than 3,000 restaurants across the U.S., including major fast food chain White Castle.[48] A mere look at its growth numbers is enough to convince one of the popularity of plant-based meat and the demand for healthier, more ethical, and more sustainable meat alternatives.

I distinctly remember trying both the Beyond burger and the Impossible burger for the first time. I was left speechless. Both burgers were juicy, tasty, and downright meaty—much like a normal beef burger. While it didn't taste *exactly* like real meat, it was delicious and I couldn't quite believe that it wasn't real meat. It seems I'm not the only one to think so. In 2018, my alma mater, Cornell University, started selling the Impossible Burger at its eateries. Since its launch, the Impossible burger has reportedly continued to rise in demand, despite its US$2 price premium compared to a beef burger. A grill-cook at Trillium, one of Cornell's eateries, tells me: "It's more expensive, but people go crazy over it."[49]

Something that always reminds me of the power of these plant-based burgers is the time when Murali Saravanan, a food writer at the *Cornell Daily Sun* (Cornell's major newspaper) tried the Impossible Burger for the first time. Murali is a major burger purist. He's such a purist, that according to him, "You don't need more than a slice of cheese, a thick patty, and a good bun."[50] So, when the Impossible burger arrived at Cornell, he was eager to review it.

In his review, he tells it like it is: "I'm going to be 100% honest with you right now—I never thought I'd eat a meatless patty that tastes as good as a beef one, but that's exactly what the Impossible Burger accomplished."[51] If a burger purist like Murali and a baby boomer meat eater like Bill Gates can be converted, so can the rest of the world.

A BETTER WAY TO (M)EAT

In a life cycle analysis study of the Beyond Burger by the University of Michigan's Center for Sustainable Systems, researchers found that the Beyond Burger generates 90% fewer greenhouse gas emissions, requires 46% less non-renewable energy, has more than 99% less impact on water scarcity, and 93% less impact on land use than a quarter pound of U.S. beef.[52] To give you an idea of the real-life impact of that, Beyond Meat gave this analogy:

"On average, Americans eat three burgers a week. If they switched just one of these beef burgers to a Beyond Burger for a year, it would be like taking 12 million cars off the road and saving enough energy to power 2.3 million homes."[53]

Now that's what I call impactful. If it wasn't already obvious, reducing your meat and dairy intake is by far the biggest way you can directly contribute to reducing your impact on climate change. While we still have a long way to go, people are increasingly becoming aware of the negative environmental effects of the traditional meat industry. Because of these growing concerns, consumers are flocking to plant-based meat substitutes that are much more environmentally sustainable than conventional meat.

Apart from sustainability concerns, another top motivator of people going more plant-based are the positive health benefits associated with plant-based foods. According to a Nielsen study of American and Canadian consumers, the top two reasons consumers want to go more plant-based were health and nutrition (83% of Americans and 85% of Canadian consumers) and weight control (62% of Americans and 56% of Canadian consumers).[54] So while plant-based foods definitely help alleviate the negative environmental impacts of conventional meat, a large majority of consumers are also going plant-based for health purposes.

These plant-based drivers have given rise to a new population of consumers called flexitarians. Flexitarians (derived from "flexible vegetarians") are either consumers who are primarily carnivores trying to add more plant-based foods into their diet or consumers who are primarily vegetarians and occasionally consume meat. Ultimately, the primary goal is to reduce meat consumption.

The emergence of flexitarianism has meant that plant-based meat's audience has expanded beyond just vegetarians and vegans. And the numbers show it. The aforementioned Nielsen global survey found that 23% of consumers worldwide want more plant-based protein on shelves.[55] Only about 3% of Impossible Foods' customers[56] and 14% of Beyond Meat customers[57] are either vegan or vegetarian. Clearly, the consumer base demanding plant-based meat products is going from a small fraction of the population to being almost a quarter of the global population. Again, the numbers don't lie.

According to Michele Simon, Executive Director of the Plant Based Foods Association (PBFA), "The plant-based foods industry has gone from being a relatively niche market to fully mainstream."[58] With consumers becoming more cognizant of the environmental and health effects of conventional meat consumption, plant-based protein alternatives may just be the stepping stone consumers need towards a more plant-based diet. If you're a big meat eater, I compel you to educate yourself about the meat you consume, and whether you can find alternatives or reduce your consumption. With a plethora of amazing plant-based meat options on the market, you might surprise yourself with how easy it is to reduce your meat intake and still meet your protein needs.

PLANT-BASED MEAT REGULATORY HURDLES

While veggie burgers and sausages have been around for years, the debate over how they can be labeled has become particularly controversial as plant-based products have grown in popularity. Just like clean meat, the plant-based meat industry has received pushback from traditional meat companies; specifically, traditional meat companies are protesting and lobbying against calling meat not derived from a live animal "meat" or "beef".

Amongst the pushback is a newly passed legislation in May 2018 that has made Missouri the first state in the U.S. to exert regulatory control over how "fake meat" products are labeled.[59] The legislation prohibits companies from "misrepresenting a product as meat that is not derived from harvested production livestock or poultry." Over in the EU, France has banned "misleading" phrases containing meat and dairy-related words such as "sausage" and "milk" from being labeled on vegetarian and vegan food products.[60]

While regulation surrounding labeling is still in murky waters, plant-based meat companies have been careful to market their products as plant-based meat alternatives. Beyond Burgers' patties are labeled "plant-based burger patties" and Impossible Foods is careful to call itself a "plant-based burger." Since these products have made it clear they are plant-based, there has been overall acceptance of these products by the U.S. FDA. For instance, in July 2018, Impossible Foods officially got the green light from the FDA declaring its patties safe to eat, creating a major win for the plant-based meat company.[61]

In the future, as long as plant-based meat companies continue to label their products clearly as plant-based, regulators have no reason to deem them guilty of exploitative or misleading marketing. Arguably, there are products labeled "organic" or "non-GMO" on the market that are even more misleading for consumers. Furthermore, while responsibility lies with producers to label products transparently, some responsibility still lies with the consumer to educate themselves about what they are buying. Specifically, consumers should be reading food ingredient labels, which is something they often fail to do. While a food name label can be misleading, ingredient labels rarely are—they are, for the most part, legally obliged to tell you exactly what is in the product.

The idea that labeling something as "Plant-Based Burger Patties" could mislead consumers into thinking it is real meat, is just plain ignorant. Consumers aren't stupid. They know almond milk is not the same as cow's milk (nor is almond milk made from lactating almonds). In the same way, they know that beef burger patties aren't the same as the Beyond Burger patty. Pushback over labeling regulation is merely the conventional meat industry's ploy to stop plant-based meat from entering the mainstream. The dairy industry tried to do the same to the plant-based dairy industry. It didn't work. From 2012 to 2017, plant-based milk sales increased by 61%, while dairy milk sales actually fell by 15%.[62] Eventually, regulators and conventional meat producers will have to wake up to the future of plant-based meat.

TRYING TO BE VEGETARIAN IN ASIA

I was born and bred in Malaysia and am ethnically Chinese. Growing up, my diet consisted of many meat-dominated dishes deriving from my Malaysian and Chinese roots. Meat-centric dishes like pork noodles, chicken rice, and beef rendang played a central role in my early food memories, as it has for many other Malaysians. If I could eat copious amounts of one food and not put on weight, I'd eat my grandma's roast pork (arguably the best in the world—I have never had such good crackling in my life and trust me, I've had a lot of crackling and roast pork).

After coming to the U.S. to pursue my undergraduate studies at Cornell University, I became more educated about the sustainability and health benefits of a plant-based diet. Not able to give up meat completely, I became a weekday vegetarian or "flexitarian" during my freshman and sophomore years. People say becoming vegetarian is hard, but it was remarkably easier than I thought. From chickpea pasta to plant-based milk ice cream, I was really spoilt for choice with the wide variety of meat-free options in America.

When I go back to Malaysia, it becomes much harder. My grandma's roast pork will always call me, and the lack of vegetarian options beyond a vegetarian pasta marinara makes it that much harder to be plant-based. As a hardcore foodie, I resort to going back to eating meat when I am home in Malaysia. However, I have hope that things can change.

In the coming years, more delicious and innovative plant-based meat and dairy alternatives will enter non-U.S. markets like Hong Kong and Singapore. It will mean that as more people see plant-based products on shelves, more people can adopt a more plant-centric diet. And as awareness of the environmental and health benefits of a plant-based diet spreads, I envision a world where it is easier for me to be vegetarian when I am back in Malaysia. I envision a shift in the meat-heavy culture embedded in many cuisines around the world. However, it will take time. Almost all cuisines around the world (except countries in South Asia like India and Nepal) have historically included meat for nutrition or cultural expression; the vegetarian and vegan diet movement often isolates traditional diets and cultures.

While plant-based products try to weave its way into global markets, the arrival of clean meat in 10-15 years will ensure that meat-heavy cuisines around the world can be more sustainable and ethical. It will mean that as fellow Malaysians and I enjoy our local meat-centric dishes like pork noodles or chicken rice, we can feel guiltless about our meat.

THE FUTURE OF MEAT

At the end of the day, meat is comprised of just five things—amino acids, lipids, water, trace minerals, and trace carbohydrates. All these components are abundant, can be sourced from plants, and can be produced without rearing animals. Plant-based meat companies like Beyond Meat have figured out how to source those core components from plants and assemble them in the structure of meat.[63] Cell-cultured meat companies like Memphis Meats are growing those core meat components outside of an animal. Without a doubt, the increasing desire to address health issues and promote environmental sustainability is spearheading a sustainable meat movement.

In the coming years, the plant-based meat trend will continue to catch on. Even Tyson, which invested in both Beyond Meat and Memphis Meats, announced in February 2019 that it will launch its own line of vegan meat.[64] The fact that one of the biggest meat producers in the world is entering the plant-based "fake meat" industry is incredibly revealing. It just goes to show how much plant-based meat is going to become commercially mainstream. To meet increasing consumer demand, plant-based meat production will increase and see unit production costs go down, making it just as cheap or cheaper than conventional meat in the near future.

In clean meat, companies like Memphis Meats will continue to find cost-efficient methods of production. Assuming clean meat doesn't meet any regulatory hurdles, we might just be a few years from clean meat being as commercially viable as conventional meat from a cost standpoint. One thing is for certain: By 2050, plant-based meat, clean meat, and conventional meat will become comparable in cost, giving us a plethora of options when it comes to meat.

While plant-based meat will be the only real vegetarian option, vegans and vegetarians who go meatless for ethical and environmental reasons—the majority—may see clean meat as a serious alternative and gravitate more towards it. Since the majority of consumers cut out meat for its unethical and unsustainable impacts, plant-based meat may just be the substitute placeholder waiting for when clean meat arrives on the shores of our shelves. Once clean meat arrives in 10-15 years, we may just see the burgeoning plant-based meat industry facing some serious competitive pressure. Personally, I believe that when the time comes, clean meat on its own will be a revolution in the food industry. Because for the first time in the food world, we'll be able to replicate real meat without the negative impacts of rearing animals. That's a crazy revelation.

The advent of affordable plant-based and clean meat is set to transform the global meat industry as we know it. These new ways of producing meat means that we can still have our meat, but also significantly reduce the overwhelming strain industrial meat production is putting on our resources. By replacing conventional meat with these meat alternatives, we can create a healthier, more humane, and sustainable food system.

Without a doubt, plant-based and clean meat will change the world. We're talking about a future where even the most dedicated vegans and vegetarians can bite into a 100% beef burger without letting go of their principles. A future where there will be almost zero chance of an animal-related E. Coli or Salmonella outbreak. A future where we can feed and meet the protein needs of our world by 2050, all while reducing the negative impacts on our planet. That is an incredibly exciting future.

PART IV

STREAMLINING THE GLOBAL FOOD SUPPLY CHAIN

CHAPTER 9

FOOD WASTE TECHNOLOGY

———

Every year, we waste enough food to feed almost 2 billion peo-ple.[1] If we reduced food waste by half, we could technically eliminate global hunger. From bio-based coatings to food waste management software, innovations in food waste man-agement are disrupting the food supply chain like never before.

"Don't finish it if you can't." My mum would often say this to me and my brothers as we were finishing up our meals. After hearing this line multiple times and realizing that I didn't need to finish everything on my plate, I became more comfortable with wasting my food.

As I started my first year of college at Cornell University, I took this food wasting habit with me. It all started with

Cornell's amazing dining halls—Cornell Dining was ranked third in Princeton Review's 2016 ranking of the Best Campus Food in America.[2] Needless to say, I was soon down the path of the infamous Freshman 15. I'd pile my plate(s) high, and whenever I took too much food—as you often do when you're faced with so many options—, I would leave whatever I couldn't finish on my plate. Little did I know that over time, this habit, along with other factors like supply chain inefficiencies, would amount to a college student like me wasting an average of 142 pounds (64 kg) of food a year.[3]

Food waste is one of the biggest yet underrated problems of the 21st century. The global cost of food wastage amounts to a shocking US$2.6 trillion a year.[4] That's almost equivalent to India's GDP. Of the US$2.6 trillion, monetary or retail costs account for US$990 billion,[5] environmental costs account for US$700 billion, and social costs account for US$900 billion.[6] The monetary or retail cost alone is projected to increase from US$990 billion to become a US$1.5 trillion problem by 2050.[7]

So when I say that food waste is one of the biggest yet underrated problems, I really mean it. Recovering just 25% of the food we waste could technically feed 870 million hungry people—effectively ending world hunger.[8] It's not quite as simple as that, but that still doesn't undermine how urgent an issue food waste is.

As if wasting food instead of feeding hungry people wasn't bad enough, food waste and loss contributes significantly to global warming; alarmingly, it generates more than 4 times as much greenhouse gas emissions as the aviation industry.[9] Up to 1.3 billion tonnes of food waste ends up in landfill every year, where it decomposes in the absence of oxygen and releases methane—a potent greenhouse gas potentially 30 times more harmful than carbon dioxide.[10]

In a world where global warming is rapidly intensifying and almost a billion people go hungry every year, food waste just doesn't make sense. It is simply one of the largest inefficiencies of our time. We produce food that is never eaten and in the process, we produce greenhouse gases and waste an immense amount of precious resources like labor, water, energy, and land. That's like burning coal that releases a ton of greenhouse gases and smoke, and then not generating any electricity from it. It's absurd.

If we didn't waste almost a third of the food we produced, then we would definitely stand a greater chance of being able to feed the world well. Instead, wasting a third of the food we produce means we often have to produce more and therefore use more resources to offset losses in our food supply chain.

"Food waste is so urgent because where and how we produce food has the biggest impact on the planet of any human activity," urges Jason Clay, senior vice president of food and markets at the World Wildlife Fund.[11] Clay is right. The biggest man-made impact on our environment is arguably our involvement and carelessness in managing food waste in our global supply chain.

So how and where does food waste and loss occur? Between harvest and consumption, food passes through a long and complex supply chain, traveling through various processing and storage facilities before ending up in the hands of retailers and consumers. Due to the perishable nature of food, food loss often occurs when there are inefficiencies in harvesting, storing, packing, or transporting food. In fact, supply chain infrastructure and efficiency alone has the potential to reduce the food losses of US$270 billion worth of food.[12]

Between all stakeholders, consumers are the single biggest culprits of food waste, contributing 42% of total food waste.[13] In that sense, the food waste problem is one of the few food problems where consumers at the end of the food chain are able to make a significant impact. Though the food waste conversation often centers around consumer behavior, it really isn't the case that all food waste occurs at the consumer level. Collectively, farms, manufacturers, and consumer-facing businesses contribute the rest of the 58% of all food waste.[14] Food producers and manufacturers still hold significant influence in both upstream and downstream of the supply chain and play a major role in reducing food waste.

Alexandria Coari, director of capital and innovation at ReFED, a U.S. nonprofit tasked with reducing food waste, agrees: "The food businesses are the ones that hold a lot of the power up and down the supply chain. They dictate what people buy at the store and the specs up and down the chain… They make the rules. We estimate that grocery retailers alone are wasting about US$18 billion worth of food annually, which is double their profits."[15]

From farm to fork, these big food companies and retailers have a hold on all stakeholders, from farmers, to legislators, and even to consumers. They dictate how food gets to us, who handles it, who grows it, where it is grown, and many more decisions beyond a consumer's control. More importantly, these large food companies have the power to make impactful change. Companies like PepsiCo and Kellogg's have the influence in scale and money to invest in new technologies that can reduce their food waste. If they choose to be, these influential companies can be significant agents of change in the fight against global food waste.

While adoption of food waste prevention innovations has traditionally been slow and developments nascent, the implementation of technologies throughout the food supply chain holds great promise for the future of food waste. From plant-based coatings around avocados to food waste management software, food waste technologies are providing novel ways of preserving food for extended shelf life and increasing the efficiency of our global food chain.

MAKING FOOD APEEL-ING

Like many others, I'm avocado obsessed. I've touched so many avocados that I can pretty much tell whether an avocado is soft enough for a guacamole or firm enough to be cut and put on a salad bowl by now. Timing is the most important thing when choosing and consuming avocados; the issue is that they ripen so damn fast.

We've all seen it before. Walk into the produce section of a grocery store and find discounted avocados as soft and sunken as a half-deflated beach ball. Cut open an avocado on the day of your Mexican taco night and find the flesh brown and disappointingly unappealing.

However, Apeel Sciences' bio-based coating is changing how long your avocados last.

Founded in 2012 with a grant from the Bill and Melinda Gates Foundation, California-based startup Apeel Sciences has invented an edible coating called Edipeel that can double the shelf life of avocados.[16] The edible coating, made of leftover plant skins and stem, slows the rate of water loss and oxidation—the two culprits of rapid produce spoilage. Beyond avocados, the company has also developed and tested skins for strawberries, bananas, mangoes, peaches, pears, nectarines, green beans, citrus fruits, and asparagus.

"The opportunity for Apeel is in addressing the 42% of overall waste that's fruits and vegetables. And that could be incredibly significant." said Chris Cochran, executive director of ReFED.[17]

With a whopping US$110 million in funding from Andreessen Horowitz, DBL Partners, and the Rockefeller and Gates foundations, Apeel Sciences's plant-based coating has incredible potential to make food significantly less perishable.[18] Using a less costly, more environmentally-friendly, and more natural way of preserving produce, Apeel's coating is slowing the decay of produce and significantly reducing food wasted post-harvest.

Apart from Apeel's solution, other novel ways of extending the shelf life of produce are emerging. Products like the FRESHGLOW Co.'s FreshPaper[19] and Hazel Technologies' 1-MCP sheets[20] consist of small, biodegradable packets that omit a vapor that delays ripening and inhibits bacterial and fungal growth. When added to produce packaging, these treated packets significantly extend the shelf life of produce. Farther Farms, another post-harvest processing technology company, has developed a novel pasteurization technique that significantly extends the shelf life and shelf stability of pre-cut fruit and vegetables.[21] This removes the need for cold storage of produce and reduces energy use throughout the supply chain, opening up new opportunities for restaurants with storage constraints.

Considering the urgency of the food waste problem, there's a major need for better post-harvest processing technologies like Apeel's and Farther Farms'. Traditional ways of food preservation like waxing produce and transporting produce in refrigerated supply chains are significantly inefficient and have an incredible environmental cost. For example, it takes 30 days for blueberries grown in Chile to travel to U.S. grocery stores.[22] To keep them fresh, farmers coat them in wax and pick them before they're even ripe. Furthermore, the berries need to be heavily refrigerated throughout its transportation, representing a significant energy and money cost.

Better post-harvest food processing technologies become even more critical when we look at which stage of the food chain food waste is most prevalent. In medium and high-income countries like the U.S. and China, food is wasted and lost mainly at later stages of the supply chain. In fact, in industrialized countries, more than 40% of losses happen at retail and consumer levels. In stark contrast, 40% of food losses occur at post-harvest and processing levels in developing countries like Vietnam and Thailand.[23] Unlike developing nations, developed countries waste large amounts of food not due to a lack of supply chain infrastructure, but due to quality standards that over-emphasize appearance. How many times have you spent 2 minutes finding a round, plump peach without imperfections or that beautiful bunch of yellow bananas? We're all guilty of it.

Emily Malina, co-founder and chief product officer of Spoiler Alert, a food waste management software company, agrees: "From our perspective, the aesthetic requirements around food is one of the leading causes of surplus and waste."[24]

By using post-harvest technologies that extend produce shelf life, food is in its "optimal" and not overripe stage longer. This increases overall appearance quality throughout the product's life cycle and reduces the waste that occurs at both the post-harvest processing and consumer retail level. With fresh fruit and vegetables accounting for more than

40% of wasted food in the U.S., it is imperative that we use these new innovations to extend the shelf life of produce and improve the quality of produce with a less carbon footprint heavy supply chain.

In the next three decades, the world is going to see post-harvest food processing technology disrupt how food gets to us and how long it lasts in our supermarkets and our homes. Post-harvest technologies like Apeel's bio-based coatings and Farther Farms' novel pasteurization process will completely revolutionize the way we preserve our produce. With such solutions, carbon-heavy cold supply chains for fresh produce will almost cease to exist. Clearly, better ways of food preservation are changing the post-harvest supply chain game. The adoption of such innovations will mean that when I walk into the supermarket's produce section, I will no longer end up disappointed with the sight of mushy, overripe avocados bound for landfill.

FOOD INSECURITY IN DEVELOPING COUNTRIES

In particular, developing countries that lack sufficient food processing infrastructure significantly feel the impacts of post-harvest food loss. As mentioned, more than 40% of fruits and vegetables in developing regions spoil before they are consumed.[25] These post-harvest losses actually reduce the income of smallholder farmers by 15%.[26] Considering the severity of post-harvest losses for farmers in developing countries, post-harvest technologies have immense implications for developing countries that lack reliable, refrigerated supply chains.

Occurring mainly at the early stages of the food value chain, overwhelming food loss is due to the lack of good storage and cooling facilities in developing nations. Consequently, the lack of cold supply chains to help maintain produce shelf life causes these countries to lose incredible amounts of their harvest, which never even make it to consumers. To address this problem, The Rockefeller Foundation launched YieldWise Food Loss in 2016, an initiative focused on reducing food loss by targeting fruits, vegetables, and staple crops in Kenya, Nigeria, and Tanzania—countries where up to half of all food grown is lost.[27] As part of the initiative, Apeel Sciences helped develop coatings for mangoes and bananas in Eastern Kenya.

"Apeel can greatly contribute to reducing those losses," says Betty Kibaara, an associate director at the Rockefeller Foundation.[28] The initiative has since indicated impressive loss reductions of 20–30%, according to maize and mango catalytic demonstrations.[29]

Solutions like coating produce post-harvest or using Farther Farms' novel pasteurization technology could do wonders in preserving produce long enough to be transported to consumers without the need for cold supply chain infrastructure. Considering that most of the world's food production growth will occur in less developed countries (LDCs) in the future, developing solutions to reduce post-harvest food losses will be integral to the continued livelihoods of food producers and farmers in LDCs.[30]

Apart from directly reducing post-harvest food losses, improving the shelf life of produce using the aforementioned technologies has great implications for reducing hunger and malnutrition in LDCs. There's a reason why you often only see non-perishable rice and pulses in food aid packages instead of nutritious fruits and vegetables. Fresh produce is simply too perishable to be shipped to disadvantaged communities that face incredible rates of malnutrition and hunger. Using innovations in food preservation, produce can be maintained long enough for it to be transported to the people that need it the most.

In the future, these post-harvest processing technologies can provide a shelf life and shelf stability that is resilient enough to safeguard incredible post-harvest food losses in developing countries. At the same time, it will help smallholder farmers bring more of their produce to market and alleviate the huge income losses experienced by these farmers. By using technology to extend the shelf life of produce, the world stands a better chance of providing nutritious produce to the nearly 2 billion people around the world who do not get enough essential vitamins and minerals to live a healthy and balanced life.[31]

THE DIGITIZATION OF FOOD WASTE MANAGEMENT

In under a year, international meal kit player HelloFresh reduced its landfill bound food waste by an impressive 65%, donating over 1 million meals in surplus food to America's food insecure.[32]

How did they do it? By partnering with Boston-based startup Spoiler Alert, a software and professional services startup that helps food businesses manage unsold inventory.[33] Using Spoiler Alert's food waste management platform, HelloFresh aggressively minimized food waste by using waste diversion and food recovery strategies to manage its surplus food.

While meal kits market themselves as reducing food waste by providing consumers with exact quantities of ingredients for a recipe, forecasting demand and supply to sufficiently fulfill every order still leads to unintended food wastage. To send exact amounts of ingredients, meal kit companies have extremely strict specifications for the size and appearance of its fresh produce. This means that while these companies work with suppliers to only source small carrots for your beef bulgogi bowl, we unfortunately do not live in a world where every carrot is 6 ounces. That means there will inevitably be food wasted.

HelloFresh admitted themselves that "although we can manage the amount of food sourced from suppliers to a certain degree, some surplus is inevitable."[34] Restaurant and food service establishments are no different. A 2014 study by the Food Waste Reduction Alliance revealed that 84% of unused food in American restaurants ends up being disposed of, with 14% being recycled and only 1% being donated.[35] A mismatch of supply and demand is a serious issue in the food chain. Inventory management is simply not effective enough.

"The first step with a lot of companies is figuring out where it's (food waste) coming from. There is this lack of coordination across the value chain, and I would argue, a lack of coordination in-house. The systems aren't talking to each other. Only once you understand where the problem is happening can you do something about it," offers Alexandria Coari, the director of capital and innovation at ReFED.[36]

Poor management of food throughout the supply chain is evidently a huge root cause of the food waste epidemic. Simply put, when supply outpaces demand, there is surplus. It's basic economics. As HelloFresh's use of Spoiler Alert has shown us, digitization offers an ideal data-driven solution to better mitigate both surpluses and deficiencies.

While Spoiler Alert's solution uses manual input entries, food inventory management will soon see the process become increasingly automated with the advancement of sensing and imaging technology. LeanPath, another food waste management software startup, is automating the process of tracking and reducing food waste. LeanPath's solution uses a smart scale and an attached tablet to weigh and code waste for the software; the software then analyzes the data and uses it to develop waste reduction strategies.[37] LeanPath's solution is so effective that it has brought on board major clients like IKEA, Aramark, Sodexo, and Google.[38]

Apart from sensing systems, the use of imaging technology to collect data on food waste is another area gaining major traction. ImpactVision, a food waste imaging company, has a solution that can tell the ripeness of an avocado without even touching it. The company uses hyperspectral imaging technology to detect the amount of dry matter in produce; the less dry matter, the riper the fruit or vegetable.[39] By using a camera to emit a particular spectrum of light on produce, an image from the light reflected back is created, revealing the produce's chemical composition. The acquired images are then processed using machine learning models and advanced analytics to reveal key food quality indicators such as the ripeness of avocados.

By using such autonomous imaging technologies, companies can more accurately decipher the condition of fruits and vegetables—something that has traditionally only been done by sight. The potential of imaging solutions is so large, that even a big grocery retailer like Wal-Mart has opted to use the technology. In 2018, Wal-Mart launched its own in-house food waste technology called Eden, an app-based software program that has analyzed more than one million photos of fresh produce to a "freshness algorithm."[40]

According to Wal-Mart's VP of Supply Chain Technology, Parvez Musani, "Eden's suite of apps helps Wal-Mart associates better monitor and care for fresh fruits and vegetables that are waiting to be shipped from distribution centers to stores. That could mean more efficiently ripening bananas, predicting the shelf life of tomatoes while they're still on the vine, or prioritizing the flow of green grocery items from the back of the store to the shelf."[41] The result of an internal hackathon amongst its merchandising team's engineers, Eden has already prevented US$86 million worth of food from being wasted.[42] In the process, Eden has turned what was once a manual food inspection process into a highly efficient and more autonomous one.

The use of advanced sensing and imaging technologies coupled by machine learning is enabling stakeholders throughout the supply chain to have unprecedented power in managing food waste. IoT enabled solutions like LeanPath's autonomous food tracking system and ImpactVision's hyperspectral imagery-based inspections will completely revolutionize how food is inspected and therefore managed. In the future, these technologies will make food inspections and food waste management more simple, efficient, and autonomous, which will hopefully incentivize more companies to reduce their waste.

A BETTER WAY TO INSPECT FOOD

My first job back in high school was as a salad artist at a health food chain called SaladStop! in Singapore. During my morning shifts, I'd help prep all the salad ingredients, chopping tomatoes and peeling boiled eggs. I distinctly remember my manager receiving shipments of fresh produce like tomatoes and avocados from various suppliers. He would roughly check the produce by visual inspection. If it looked good, he would sign off the invoice. If it didn't look good, he would reject the supplier's produce. Because he didn't have time to check through every single piece of produce in the delivery, we would often find several rotten tomatoes or overripe avocados in the shipment, which ultimately ended up being wasted.

Finding bad produce or rejecting bad produce is not uncommon in the food industry. There's an urgent need to discover more accurate and efficient ways to detect food spoilage earlier. Currently, the conventional way that produce is inspected is by sight or by touch. That's an awfully subjective way to judge something objective—whether a piece of fruit has nearly spoiled or not. It's like buying a designer dress or suit without first trying it on and deciding if it fits or not.

Armed with advanced imaging and sensing solutions, the digitization of food waste management will allow us to better detect early signs of produce decay and better mitigate food waste. Ultimately, we'll be able to automate the entire process of food inspection and make produce quality assessments more accurate than what my manager at SaladStop! did.

When I think about the huge implications of digitizing our food chains, much like the use of drones in early disease detection, I draw parallels to how the Internet of Things shaped the field of predictive maintenance in manufacturing; the digitization of machinery has allowed breakdowns to be detected before they actually cause production to halt (a costly consequence). Similarly, digitizing our food supply chain from harvest to consumer is incredibly important in the early detection and reduction of potential food waste. Not only will digitization help us mitigate food waste, it will bring a level of visibility and traceability to our food chains like never before.

THE FUTURE OF FOOD WASTE TECHNOLOGY

Food waste is one of the most pervasive issues the food and agriculture industry is facing. The greatest paradox is that while 821 million people go hungry every year, we waste 30-40% of the food we produce that could go to feeding these hungry people. Again, let me be clear. If we saved the 30-40% of the food we already produce, we could technically direct all that salvaged food to solving world hunger.

If we are to feed the world nutritionally well by 2050, extending the shelf life of our produce should be high on the agenda. A core component of that agenda is the use of food waste technologies to tackle the global food waste epidemic. Food waste innovations like Apeel Sciences' bio-based coating and ImpactVision's hyperspectral imagery-based inspections will ensure that food gets to the people that need it before it's too late. Along with severely reducing food waste, these technologies will also help developing nations safeguard more produce and ultimately bring an end to carbon-heavy cold supply chains.

Evidently, the food waste technologies explored in this chapter have significant implications for our fight against food waste. As mentioned, supply chain infrastructure and efficiency alone has a major role to play in reducing food waste and loss; it has the potential to save US$270 billion worth of food.[43] That's enough to feed 72 million families of 4 in South Africa nutritionally well for a year, according to the Pietermaritzburg Agency for Community Social Action (PACSA) minimum nutrition food basket index.[44]

The food supply chain is experiencing a major technological disruption for the better. Just like how big data and analytics digitized the factory and is digitizing the farm, it is also digitizing the entire food supply chain. Armed with novel innovations and sensing and imaging capabilities at our fingertips, food waste management will become increasingly autonomous, objective, and standardized. Put simply, these technological innovations will bring greater visibility to the food supply chain, paving the way for better food waste management.

It's about time we paid more attention to the food that is being lost and wasted throughout our global supply chain. That means it's about time we embrace innovative food waste technologies. Ultimately, we'll need these technologies and innovative ways of thinking to save the food the world needs and deserves.

CHAPTER 10

THE DIGITIZATION OF THE FOOD SUPPLY (BLOCK)CHAIN

—

Hype or hope? The blockchainization of food provenance is reinventing the global food supply chain. In food we trust.

Imagine being able to trace the source and conditions of a piece of fresh fruit or vegetable from the farm where it was produced to the store where it ended up in a mere 2.2 seconds.[1]

That's what Wal-Mart and IBM's enterprise-ready, blockchain traceability solution called IBM Food Trust was able to do. That's what the future of supply chains will look like.

Before using the blockchain, it took Wal-Mart approximately 6 days, 18 hours, and 26 minutes to trace a package of sliced mangoes grown in Mexico.[2] Blockchain not only cut that time down to an unprecedented 2.2 seconds, it also allowed Wal-Mart to obtain unique information that was previously unavailable—information like the fact that there was four days of bottleneck due to the shipment being held up at the U.S. border. Wal-Mart could also see audit certificates and other food safety-related documents attached to the product, all of which helped improve the efficiency of its transportation.[3]

Frank Yiannas, Wal-Mart's VP of food safety, spoke to the future of the blockchain in the food system: "blockchain is ushering in a new era of food transparency," noting that Wal-Mart's test with IBM Food Trust allowed the mega-retailer to achieve traceability at the "speed of thought."[4] Yiannas asserts that "blockchain has the potential to be a light shining on all nodes in the food system. That transparency leads to accountability, and accountability leads to responsibility."[5]

What Yiannas is alluding to is that greater transparency in food supply chains is incredibly significant. Essentially, it enables *all* stakeholders to quickly obtain important and accurate information about a food chain. Information like Wal-Mart's four-day bottleneck at the U.S. border is critical to understanding how and where food waste could be reduced. Information like when the produce was harvested is important to accurately evaluate when the produce will start to spoil. With such information, the root causes of food waste can be identified and better mitigated. Currently, such information isn't readily available to all stakeholders in the food chain.

Blockchain makes this critical information available to every single stakeholder. Yes, blockchain—the technology that has gained enormous hype, especially in Bitcoin and cryptocurrencies. Aside from disruptive applications in finance, blockchain has a key role to play in reducing food supply chain inefficiency and improving food safety and verification in the agri-food sector.

DIGITIZING FOOD PROVENANCE

So what exactly is the blockchain? What about it makes it indispensable in the future of transparent food chains? Simply put, blockchain technology is a way of storing and sharing information across a network of users in an open virtual space.[6] It is a public ledger of every single past transaction, all the way back to the very first Bitcoin payment made on the blockchain. The blockchain's transaction history is locked in and secured by cryptography, a form of encrypting transactions and information using a series of mathematical algorithms. This makes a blockchain's transactions and information very secure and extremely hard to tamper with.[7]

One of the blockchain's key characteristics is that it is decentralized and therefore, public. Instead of transactions and information on the blockchain being stored in one central location, as current computer servers operate, it is distributed to every user in the blockchain network. By creating a truly public ledger, fraud is significantly reduced since every entity or transaction on the blockchain carries its original history with it. This means in order to even attempt to replicate something like a bitcoin, you would need to completely recreate a lineage of its past transactions since the beginning. Even so, doing this would not work, since the millions of transactions on the ledger stored throughout the rest of the network would not have any record of this counterfeit transaction nor its invented history. Your counterfeit bitcoin transaction would immediately be detected and rejected.[8]

Essentially, blockchain as a widely distributed ledger works to decentralize digital trust. With blocks of information cryptographically locked so that only data owners and those they give permission to can access it, privacy can also be maintained on the blockchain.[9] Yet, a significant level of transparency in the accuracy and traceability of information is available. In essence, the blockchain is unique in that it can provide both privacy and transparency simultaneously.

Beyond the Bitcoin hype, the biggest opportunity for the blockchain will be to bring greater transparency and unprecedented levels of traceability to the global food chain. Because the blockchain ensures an immutable digital record of transactions, it is ideal for tracing the safety and authenticity of food as it moves from farm, to supplier, to store shelves, and to consumers. While there are big implications for food safety in terms of quick detection of a foodborne outbreak, increased transparency will also play a major role in reducing the pervasive issue of food waste. As mentioned before, much of the food chain's food waste can be traced back to inconsistencies and inefficiencies in the food chain.

Ultimately, the blockchain allows every stakeholder—from farmer, to supplier, to distributor, to retailer—to track the conditions and history of food to ensure successful handling and delivery. Instead of recalling all products suspected of being contaminated, easy and quick traceability in the supply blockchain will objectively allow only food safe products to remain on shelves and not be sent to landfill.

For example, transactions of avocados on the blockchain would allow retailers to have highly accurate and verified information about whom the avocado supplier has dealt with, the conditions of the avocados at each processing stage, and where any roadblocks occurred. With all this information, the blockchain gives all stakeholders an unprecedented 360° view of the avocado's lifecycle, allowing bottlenecks to be identified quickly. By knowing the conditions of avocados received, retailers and distributors can better allocate inventory and mitigate potential wastage.

In a food supply blockchain world, retailers will be armed with the information to allocate a section of avocados ripe enough to consume today, a section to be consumed in the next 2-3 days, and a section to be consumed in a week. All this would play a key role in both mitigating waste and meeting unique consumer needs. If you've ever gone to the grocery store with the intention of making some guacamole that same day, you'll know how valuable this is. The same can be done with bananas, peaches, plums, tomatoes—the list goes on. In essence, this sort of traceability and transparency will radically reduce how much food is unsold and therefore wasted in supermarkets.

As the blockchain becomes less nascent and more adoptable, it will form a key part of the food chain's future infrastructure—infrastructure required to facilitate the great efficiencies desperately needed to cut global food waste.

MORE EFFICIENCIES, LESS INTERMEDIARIES

In December 2017, Louis Dreyfus Co. (LDC), one of the world's leading agricultural commodities traders, completed the world's first commodity trade using the blockchain.[10] LDC trialed the blockchain-based digital platform for the sale of 60,000 tonnes of U.S. soybeans to China's Shandong Bohi Industry Co. In a shocking turn of events, the use of the blockchain cut the entire transaction time down by 80%.[11]

"Our expectations were high, but the results were even higher," gushed Robert Serpollet, global head of trade operations at LDC.[12]

One of the underlying reasons for the astounding decrease in transaction time was due to the use of digitized documents and real-time data verification to facilitate the deal.[13] Since documents provided on the blockchain were highly reliable and verified, intermediaries like distributors or commodity traders did not need to manually check relevant trade documentation. Without the need to manually verify trade documentation like the sales contract, letter of credit, and government certifications, many back office processes were eliminated and the entire process was streamlined.[14]

Automatically matching data in real time and removing manual checks meant that LDC's trade could happen more quickly on the blockchain, where documentation is securely and accurately verified, than off the blockchain. For other commodity supply chains, this means that trades can happen much quicker and food can be moved around faster and more efficiently, getting to consumers before it has a chance to spoil and end up as waste.

Karin Kersten, global head of trade & commodity finance at Dutch Bank ABN Amro, helped facilitate LDC's trade and is optimistic about the use of blockchain technology in food commodities trading: "We not only proved that this blockchain transaction is technically possible, but also that it yields what it promises. The trade saved labor and time, but also reduced the risk of fraud or human errors."[15]

Anthony van Vliet, Global Head of Trade Commodities at the Dutch bank ING Group, also helped facilitate LDC's trade and emphasized that "the cost benefits are significant. It's clear that a traditional, somewhat old-fashioned industry working with largely paper documents needs a bit of a digital upgrade."[16]

The imminent reduction of intermediaries throughout a food supply blockchain also means that food prices will go down without third party markups. Lower overall costs will eventually bring down the retail price of food, increasing the accessibility to nutritious foods—especially for low-to-middle income households.

As LDC's trade and Wal-Mart and IBM's blockchain project has shown us, a food supply blockchain not only ensures greater transparency and traceability in the food chain, it also vastly increases efficiency by reducing transaction costs and time. The fact of the matter is that our global food chain is highly complex; it involves farmers, shipping companies, distributors, and retailers who rarely all use the same record keeping method. Instead of using a combination of apps, legacy software systems, spreadsheets, and pen and paper to keep records, the blockchain acts as a *single* database for stakeholders throughout the supply chain. That completely eliminates the need to maintain multiple record systems and save valuable time and energy in the value chain.

The future of food chains exists on the blockchain. With the need to nourish almost 10 billion people by 2050, larger shipments of food and agricultural commodities will become increasingly ubiquitous. Currently, such transactions are incredibly complex, with multiple intermediaries involved in payment and transfer of ownership. The blockchain removes all that complexity, making way for faster and more efficient food supply chains.

PARTICIPATION, PARTICIPATION, PARTICIPATION

Despite the multitude of benefits offered by food supply blockchains, the application of the blockchain in food supply chains still faces limitations and challenges. Amongst all challenges, the most important challenge for blockchain adoption is still participation. Ultimately, the food supply blockchain can only work if *all* stakeholders throughout the supply chain use the technology.

While industry-wide adoption is critically necessary, it is currently still lacking due to challenges like the lack of standardized platforms and systems. Technical challenges like managing the interoperability of data platforms remain barriers for widespread participation. However, with rapid developments in platform integration and infrastructure, these are technical issues that I am confident the blockchain industry will be able to solve in the next 5—10 years.

In considering participation on the blockchain, large food companies that currently use their power to heavily influence the food chain could actually find issue with the fact that information is highly transparent and easily accessible on the blockchain.[17] While a major benefit, increased transparency may actually deter these large food companies from fully participating, for fear of revealing too much information. For instance, transaction information relating to how much a retailer purchased a product would essentially reveal the retailer's margins for that product. This could be problematic, because such a level of information symmetry could potentially ruin consumers' perceptions and negatively affect purchasing behavior.

Despite this, there seems to be growing participation from retailers and suppliers in the food supply blockchain. IBM Food Trust, IBM's food traceability blockchain platform, saw its pilot phase from 2017 to 2018 tracking millions of food products with participation from some of the world's biggest retailers and suppliers, including Wal-Mart, Nestlé, Unilever, Kroger, Driscoll's, Dole, Tyson Foods, and many more.[18] Encouragingly, Wal-Mart, the biggest retailer in the world and one of the founding members of IBM Food Trust, announced in September 2018 that it would launch the Walmart Food Traceability Initiative—a food safety program that requires suppliers of fresh leafy greens to use the IBM Food Trust network to capture digital, end-to-end traceability information.[19] At this rate of participation, food supply blockchain adoption looks optimistic.

Despite all the encouraging developments we're seeing in the adoption of blockchain in the food supply chain, the technology is really still in its infancy and many are still skeptical and cautious of its adoption. Especially with the confusion and skepticism surrounding Bitcoin, many still see blockchain technology as irrational and quite frankly, ridiculous. Many stakeholders, including governments, are still struggling to grasp how the technology could even work in a decentralized system. Thus, participation and the need to solve technical challenges will still be critical barriers for several years before widespread adoption.

Despite the limitations and challenges, rapid developments in blockchain infrastructure and increasing alignment with business and government agendas will eventually lead the way for food supply blockchain adoption by 2050. Like any disruptive novel technology, skepticism rules until pragmatism is realized. Eventually, the overwhelming benefits of such a distributed ledger system will be evident, allowing it to drastically improve the efficiency and traceability of global food supply chains.

THE FUTURE OF THE FOOD SUPPLY (BLOCK)CHAIN

Hope or hype, the blockchain is undoubtedly disrupting global food supply chains. The ability to monitor a supply chain's progress in real time, verify data accuracy, and reduce fraud risk are key characteristics that will drive the blockchain to transform the agricultural supply chain. Perfect transparency and increased efficiency will mean greater opportunities to mitigate waste by identifying bottlenecks that cause food waste and loss. At the same time, it will mean greater opportunities to remove intermediaries and reduce transaction costs and obsolete paper work.

Ed Treacy, vice president of supply chain efficiencies for the Produce Marketing Association, summarizes the great opportunities offered by the blockchain:

"Blockchain holds the potential to help us be more transparent and transform how the food industry works by speeding up investigations into contaminated food, authenticating the origin of food, and providing insights about the conditions and pathway the food traveled to identify opportunities to maximize shelf life and reduce losses due to spoilage."[20]

If we are to "halve per capita global food waste at the retail and consumer level, and reduce food losses along production and supply chains by 2030," an objective under the UN Sustainable Development Goal #12, we need to understand precisely how and where food waste and loss occurs.[21] Building on the digitization of food waste management through IoT, the use of the blockchain will create a truly transparent and highly efficient end-to-end food chain.

CONCLUSION

THE FUTURE OF FOOD DISRUPTION

In the coming decades, food will undoubtedly continue to be one of the most important industries in the world, with significant innovation opportunities for how food is produced, processed, transported, and received. In the face of pressing global issues like hunger and climate change, we must be able to nourish almost 10 billion people by 2050 while meeting climate and environmental impact goals. While food and agriculture is not the only avenue to achieving climate goals like the Paris Agreement's, it is certainly a vital contributor to meeting these goals.

Despite the challenges that the future of food production will face, we are living in an incredible time. The rapid development and commoditization of big data, sensors, and AI is giving farmers the ability to better predict and optimize farm management. Autonomous systems are replacing the menial and laborious tasks of farmers. Indoor farm technology is unlocking opportunities in vertical farming, expanding food production from rural areas to urban cities. Breakthrough discoveries in gene editing and cellular agriculture are helping us re-engineer our food, creating the world's most resilient crops and meat that we can feel good about. Food waste technologies and the blockchain are rapidly digitizing and streamlining our global food supply chains.

The exponential pace of technological innovation has meant that we're now able to make the impossible possible. If you asked anyone ten years ago if humans could produce real meat without rearing a live animal, they would have told you you're absolutely insane. But time and again, the sweeping innovations of the food and agriculture industry have shown us that sustainable disruption will happen. It must happen and it is happening. Right now.

THE FOURTH AGRICULTURAL REVOLUTION

The rapid advancement of farming technology, food science, and digital devices has transitioned humankind to the next agricultural revolution—the Fourth Agricultural Revolution. How did we get here?

The First Agricultural Revolution marked the fundamental transition from hunting and gathering food to cultivating food for human consumption.

The Second Agricultural Revolution of the 18th and 19th centuries were marked by mass mechanization and farm commercialization, shifting farming from manual labor to horse labor to machine labor.

The Green Agricultural Revolution, or the Third Agricultural Revolution, was marked by mass agrochemical use, crop breeding techniques, and intensive cultivation methods that drastically increased crop yields, though at the cost of the environment and the health of humans.

The Fourth Agricultural Revolution? We've already entered it. Marked by the integration of new innovations, the Fourth Agricultural Revolution will see us using technology to meet our global food and health demands, all whilst ensuring we reduce the negative environmental effects of agriculture. Innovations in precision agriculture, novel farming systems, gene-editing, cellular agriculture, and food waste management will disrupt the entire food chain, bringing drastic changes like never before.

THE 6 D'S OF EXPONENTIALS

In thinking about disruption in the future of food and agriculture, Ben and Sam from the Small Robot Company kindly pointed me towards the 6Ds of Exponentials, a critical framework for understanding and planning for disruption in any industry.[1]

According to Peter Diamandis and Steven Kotler, co-authors of *Bold: How to Go Big, Create Wealth and Impact the*

World: "The Six Ds are a chain reaction of technological progression, a road map of rapid development that always leads to enormous upheaval and opportunity."[2]

I find it fitting to use this framework to better understand future disruptions in food and agriculture. The first D, is digitized. In this stage, digital information is easy to access, share, and distribute.[3] On the farm, the IoT, data analytics, and autonomous systems provide farmers easy access to smart and actionable data. In the food supply chain, food waste management software is digitizing food waste, providing a highly efficient way of managing and minimizing waste. In an industry that has traditionally lacked digitization, food and agriculture is *hungry* for it.

The second D, is deceptive. This is when something has an initial period of growth that is wildly deceptive due to the nature of exponential growth initially being mild.[4] If you think back to high school algebra, exponential growth only really takes off after the whole number barrier is surpassed. Once that barrier is overcome, then disruption really starts to skyrocket. I consider industries like agricultural drones and CRISPR in the deceptive stages, because once barriers like regulation are overcome, these industries will rise to the challenge.

You may well guess that the third D, is disruption. This is when an existing industry is suddenly shaken by a new solution or a new market.[5] If you can buy clean beef that is as delicious, cheap, and more sustainable than Angus beef, then why buy Angus beef? If you can buy hydroponically-grown lettuce that travelled fewer miles, retained more nutrients, and grew with fewer inputs, then why buy soil-grown lettuce? While not all agri-food technologies have exactly skyrocketed yet, by 2050, they will reach the exponent of 1 and take off.

The fourth D, is demonetized—when the technology becomes much cheaper.[6] Many see this stage as commoditization. By 2050, precision farming tools and robots will become so developed that they become near commodities to farmers. By 2050, alternative meat products will be as commercially viable as conventional meat, becoming highly affordable and accessible to consumers. By 2050, food waste technologies will become so common that producers, distributors (will they still exist in 2050?), and retailers won't even think twice about using them.

The last two Ds, are dematerialized and democratized—when technologies that were once bulky and expensive become more compact and portable, and therefore accessible to the masses.[7] Today, farm management systems still involve bulky tractors equipped with controllers. In a dematerialized world, you could manage an entire farm armed with autonomous robots from your mobile phone. Would a farmer even need to be on the farm?

Realistically, some agri-food technologies will never make it to the last stages of dematerialization and democratization due to the implicit nature of these technologies. For instance, vertical farms will never get to the last two

Ds because of the nature of such an innovation. Some, like precision farming tools and drones, easily will. One thing is for sure—disruptions in the global agri-food industry *will* happen.

A big concern of all this disruption is how sustainable it is. The full implications of transforming the human-driven activities of food production to non-human, digital platforms are relatively unexplored. Fundamental challenges like farmer displacement and regulation lie ahead for these technological innovations. Facing these challenges won't be easy, but they sure as hell are worth it.

In order to create sustainable change, I believe everyone must come together to tackle these challenges head on. From farmers, to distributors, to restaurateurs, to scientists, to consumers, the future of food requires collaboration and understanding.

FUTURE FOOD DISRUPTORS: CONGLOMERATES VS. STARTUPS

As with any disruptive innovations, there will be those who embrace and those who resist agri-food technologies. Unfortunately, those who resist and ignore these technological innovations will fall behind, just as Kodak did in digital cameras and photography. Realistically, less technologically adept stakeholders in the food and agriculture industry will eventually have their work rendered obsolete, while food disruptors that embrace technology will prevail.

For the most part, the food disruptors that are shaping the future of food and agriculture are nimble startups at the forefront of novel technological innovations. Whether in cell-cultured meat or CRISPR, risk-averse agri-food conglomerates will soon see themselves falling behind. Meanwhile, innovative startups will move fast and provide more high quality, sustainable, and efficient solutions. For instance, Tyson, one of the biggest meat producers in the world, could never have anticipated that Beyond Meat's plant-based meat patties would achieve such success in the market. Certainly, they could not have imagined that a small startup like Memphis Meats would be able to produce meat without rearing a live animal.

Clearly, power is shifting from large agri-food conglomerates to nimble and innovative startups. Powerful technologies that were once only available to large corporations and governments are becoming more affordable and accessible than ever. Thus, the potential for forward-thinking entrepreneurs and tech-savvy companies to disrupt food and for large agri-food conglomerates to fall behind has never been greater.

The old saying applies: If you can't beat them, join them.

"The startup companies are the ones who are the big risk takers, but then the bigger companies come and buy them out. The big story for the private sector is that because there's so much startup activity now, there's lots of new innovations coming from biotechnology, genomics, food science, and food safety, that the big private companies have a lot more opportunities to grow from these innovations," offers Dr. Prabhu Pingali.[8]

As Dr. Pingali suggests, big agri-food conglomerates will eventually line up to acquire these innovative startups. In fact, the competition towards the future is so fast and fierce, that large agri-businesses like Monsanto and Cargill have already invested in or bought out promising startups, instead of trying to compete themselves.

Like many other industries, the future landscape of food and agriculture will take on a completely different look and feel. While large agri-food companies shaped the sweeping innovations of the last agricultural revolution, almost all the companies I've highlighted in this book have been of relatively young startups working on cutting-edge innovations. Clearly, it no longer takes a huge agri-food company to make huge impact. That's incredibly exciting.

FACING CHANGE

While I speak of sweeping technological disruption, I am also cognizant of the importance of nature, tradition, and instinct in food production. Some of the tech-driven trends mentioned in this book, like the rise of urban agriculture using indoor farm technology, inadvertently conflicts with traditional farmer values like respecting the land on which food is produced. In Dan Barber's powerful book *The Third Plate*, he discusses the culture of the *dehesa,* a forest landscape in Spain best known for grazing Iberian pigs for Jamón Ibérico.[9]

Drawing upon the concept of land ethics in the connection between man and land, Barber quotes conservationist writer Aldo Leopold: "That land is a community is the basic concept of ecology, but that land is to be loved and respected is an extension of ethics." Barber affirms that "farmers are raised to respect the land as nearly sacred ground."[10]

I do not disrespect all this for one second. I have a deep admiration for farmers who work with our land, soil, and seas to provide nourishment for the world. So, to ask farmers to put technology above their values rooted in tradition, may be deeply controversial. Some argue that digitizing and automating the farm is the antithesis of the concept of cultivating land for food. However, if industries like entertainment and media and stories like Kodak's downfall have taught me anything, it's that if you do not adapt, you die. If we are to nourish 10 billion people by 2050, and do so while meeting our global environmental and economic goals, great change *must* happen.

In line with Barber and Leopold's views, I agree you can't fight or deny nature and ecology. Nature and ecology will always work as it sees best and it may not adapt to us—we must adapt to it. This may seem like a book all about how technology will solve all our problems, but I don't wholly think so. Food and agriculture is much more complicated than that. Technology is part of the solution, not the entire solution. Changing perceptions of what good food is, how we access and grow our food, and what we vote for with our forks is equally important.

HOPE

Some would say I am over-optimistic about the role of technological innovation in the future of food and agriculture. Perhaps I am, but I am not oblivious to the consequences of such disruption. I know that the disruptive changes explored in this book can be daunting and met with apprehension (I will never forget when one of my editors, Andrew, commented on my chapter on sustainable meat: "Is there a better word than brewery? Because honestly the word meat brewery just sounds gross.") I know that the future of food and agriculture technology will face a multitude of challenges. I know that some farmers will probably be left behind. I know all this. Yet, I am still optimistic. I am optimistic, because I truly believe that the future of food and agriculture can only change with groundbreaking and deeply anti-institutional innovation. Considering the challenges that food and agriculture will increasingly face, what we need most of all, is *hope*.

A great story of hope is in my conversations with entrepreneurs and innovators in food and agriculture. Something that almost always comes up is the difficulty of getting farmers and producers to adopt new technological solutions. One challenge is that the majority of farmers are of the baby boomer population and are extremely risk-averse when adopting new technology. Another challenge is that many of these solutions are currently too expensive for small-to-medium farmers.

While this all sounds discouraging, you'd be surprised how these conversations end. They always end with hope. Hope that some of these technologies can be adapted and scaled down to increase its accessibility and affordability. Hope that a new generation of tech-savvy, modern farmers will embrace these innovations. Again, hope. Hope is everything for the future of food and agriculture. Because while great challenges and uncertainties lie ahead of food and agriculture, it doesn't stop us from seeing the future.

The future of food and agriculture is a deeply powerful, fundamental, and impactful one. It is a future that is fighting and working for a better, more equal, and more sustainable food system. It's a future I will be working relentlessly on shaping and fixing. I hope it's a future you aim to shape too.

ACKNOWLEDGEMENTS

I owe a debt of gratitude to Eric Koester, who gave me an opportunity of a lifetime. Getting a LinkedIn message from you last summer was the most random blessing, but it turned my life upside down (in a good way). I am incredibly glad to have witnessed your voracious drive, entrepreneurial talent, and crazy optimism. You have showed me the value of creation and inspired me in countless ways.

My gratitude goes to Laurel Hecker, who has poured over every sentence in this book and been so indispensable in this journey. Laurel, your emoji-filled comments made many days better and improved this book in countless ways. Your sustained attention, coaching, and copious editing shaped this book to what it is today. You are the best developmental editor a first-time author could ask for.

And to the rest of my New Degree Press team—Brian Bies, Maylon Gardner, Andrew Pourciax, Srdjan Filipovic, Liana Moisescu, Gina Champagne, and Lyn Solares—thank you. It takes a village to publish a book. This book would not be here without all of you.

Words cannot explain how thankful I am to Amy Newman, who offered her wisdom, judgement, and loving support since the early days of writing this book. Amy, you are a phenomenal teacher and a great friend. You contributed more to this book than you know.

I have much to thank for the people who have been so generous in offering their insights and information in conversations and email exchanges. Much of what I know about food and agriculture tech is because of the fearless and inspirational work you all do. Thank you to Michael Eaton, Simon Roberts, Jack Roswell, Mike Beveridge, Katherine Muller, Kristen Yi, Rod Hawkes, Nikunj Beria, Steven James, Mike Hoffman, Andrew Novakovic, Barak Cohen, Kirk Haney, Kisum Chan, Ben Scott-Robinson, Sam Watson Jones, Darren Ho, Jan Nyrop, Jill Gould, Kristen Barnett, Lucy Best, Owen Hoekenga, Christine Gould, Joseph Shen, Neil Mattson, Adam Fine, Phaedra Randolph, Stephen Frattini, Joyce Van Eck, Shannon Theobald, Hod Lipson, Aylon Steinhart, Haiyan Cen, and David Benzaquen. Thank you especially to Prabhu Pingali, for his continued support and guidance.

Writing a book is not an easy ride, but I am lucky to have some of the greatest friends that offer the most incredible support for all my crazy projects, including this book. The countless words of encouragement and strong belief in me made my days of writing this book much better. There are many of you to thank, but you know who you are.

I must acknowledge my dearest friends, Yeshey Seldon and Kristie Lui, who have been sounding boards for my crazy ideas and my soul sisters for many years now. Seldon and Kristie, your generous love, unwavering support, and inspirational kindness makes me the luckiest girl in the world. I don't know what I did to deserve the most amazing and beautiful people to call my best friends.

And last but not least, my parents—my pillars. Thank you to my mum, who has done everything she can to make every opportunity available to me and has always encouraged me to explore what I am most passionate about. Thank you to my dad, who has *literally* shown me what hard work, discipline, and resilience is. You've both shaped the person I am today and I am forever grateful for that.

NOTES

PREFACE: THE FUTURE OF FOOD MISSION

1. Adam Andrzejewski, *Harvesting U.S. Farm Subsidies* (OpenTheBooks. com, 2018), 2.

2. Brian Riedl, "How Farm Subsidies Harm Taxpayers, Consumers, And Farmers, Too," *The Heritage Foundation*, June 19, 2007, https://www.heritage.org/agriculture/report/ how-farm-subsidies-harm-taxpayers-consumers-and-farmers-too.

INTRODUCTION: NOURISHING THE WORLD IN 2050

1. Frank Viviano, "This Tiny Country Feeds the World," National Geographic, September 2017, https://www.nationalgeographic.com/ magazine/2017/09/holland-agriculture-sustainable-farming/.

2. Viviano, "This Tiny Country Feed the World."

3. McDonald's Flagship Farms, *Potatoes – Van Den Borne, Netherlands*, (Netherlands: McDonald's Flagship Farms, 2017), 7.

4. "World Population Projected to Reach 9.8 Billion In 2050, And 11.2 Billion In 2100," *UN DESA (United Nations Department Of Economic And Social Affairs)*, June 21, 2017, https://www.un.org/development/desa/en/news/population/world-population-prospects-2017.html.

5. Sam Meredith, "Two-Thirds Of Global Population Will Live In Cities By 2050, UN Says", *CNBC*, May 17, 2018, https://www.cnbc.com/2018/05/17/two-thirds-of-global-population-will-live-in-cities-by-2050-un-says.html.

6. FAO, *Global Agriculture Towards 2050*, How To Feed The World 2050 (Rome: FAO, 2009), http://www.fao.org/fileadmin/templates/wsfs/docs/Issues_papers/HLEF2050_Global_Agriculture.pdf.

7. FAO, IFAD, UNICEF, WFP and WHO, *The State of Food Security and Nutrition in the World* (Rome: FAO, 2018), 5.

8. FAO, IFAD, UNICEF, WFP and WHO, *The State of Food Security and Nutrition in the World*, 5.

9. "Know Your World: Facts About Hunger and Poverty," *The Hunger Project*, last updated November 2017, https://www.thp.org/knowledge-center/know-your-world-facts-about-hunger-poverty/.

10. The Hunger Project, "Know Your World."

11. Eric Holt-Giménez et al., "We Already Grow Enough Food For 10 Billion People … And Still Can't End Hunger," *Journal of Sustainable Agriculture* 36, no. 6 (July 2012): 595-598, doi:10.1080/10440046.2012.695331.

12. "Food Loss and Food Waste," *FAO*, accessed February 21, 2019, http://www.fao.org/food-loss-and-food-waste/en

13. Holt-Giménez et al., "We Already Grow Enough Food," 595-598.

14. Neil Palmer, "Making Climate Finance Work in Agriculture", *World Bank*, accessed 21 February 2019, http://www.worldbank.org/en/topic/agriculture/publication/making-climate-finance-work-in-agriculture.

15. "Global Greenhouse Gas Emissions Data," *U.S. EPA (United States Environmental Protection Agency)*, accessed February 21, 2019, https://www.epa.gov/ghgemissions/global-greenhouse-gas-emissions-data.

16. Sonja J. Vermeulen, Bruce M. Campbell and John S.I. Ingram, "Climate Change and Food Systems", *Annual Review Of Environment And Resources* 37, no. 1 (November 2012): 195-222, doi:10.1146/annurev-environ-020411-130608.

17. Joseph Poore and Thomas Nemecek, "Reducing Food's Environmental Impacts Through Producers And Consumers", *Science* 360, no. 6392 (2018): 987-992, doi:10.1126/science.aaq0216.

18. GRAIN and the IATP (Institute of Agriculture and Trade Policy), *Emissions impossible: how big meat and dairy are heating up the planet* (GRAIN and IATP, 2018), 2.

19. Josh Gabbatiss, "Meat and Dairy Companies To Surpass Oil Industry As World's Biggest Polluters", *The Independent*, July 18, 2018, https://www.independent.co.uk/environment/meat-dairy-industry-greenhouse-gas-emissions-fossil-fuels-oil-pollution-iatp-grain-a8451871.html.

20. Gabbatiss, "Meat and Dairy."

21. "The Paris Agreement," *United Nations Climate Change*, last updated October 22, 2018, https://unfccc.int/process-and-meetings/the-paris-agreement/the-paris-agreement.

22. Chad Frischmann, "The Climate Impact of The Food in The Back Of Your Fridge", *The Washington Post*, July 31, 2018, https://www.washingtonpost.com/news/theworldpost/wp/2018/07/31/food-waste/.

23. FAO, *Food Wastage Footprint & Climate Change* (Rome: FAO, 2018), 1.

24. "Summary of Solutions by Overall Rank," *Drawdown*, accessed February 21, 2019, https://www.drawdown.org/solutions-summary-by-rank.

25. "Goal 2: Zero Hunger," *United Nations Sustainable Development Goals*, accessed February 21, 2019, https://www.un.org/sustainabledevelopment/hunger/.

26. "Neolithic Revolution," *HISTORY*, January 12, 2018, https://www.history.com/topics/pre-history/neolithic-revolution.

27. Mary Bellis, "History of The Agricultural Revolution," *ThoughtCo.*, May 22, 2018, https://www.thoughtco.com/agricultural-revolution-1991931.

28. Bellis, "History of The Agricultural Revolution."

29. Bellis, "History of The Agricultural Revolution."

30. Bellis, "History of The Agricultural Revolution."

31. Bellis, "History of The Agricultural Revolution."

32. Amanda Briney, "All You Wanted to Know About the Green Revolution," *ThoughtCo.*, January 13, 2019, https://www.thoughtco.com/green-revolution-overview-1434948.

33. Henry Kindall and David Pimentel, "Constraints On The Expansion of The Global Food Supply," *Ambio* 23, no. 3 (May 1994): 198-205.

34. Gordan Conway, *One Billion Hungry: Can We Feed the World?* (New York: Cornell University Press, 2012), 41-53.

35. Conway, *One Billion Hungry*, 41-53.

36. Yeow Chor Lee, Conversation with author, December 4, 2018.

37. FAO, *Global Agriculture Towards 2050*.

38. Louisa Burwood-Taylor, "What Is Agrifood Tech?" *AgFunder News*, August 15, 2017, https://agfundernews.com/what-is-agrifood-tech.html.

CHAPTER 1: THE AGE OF SMART AGRICULTURE

1. "Kickin' Up The Dirt With Keith Gingerich," *The Dirt*, November 11, 2016, https://dirtforfarmers.com/kickin-up-the-dirt-with-keith-gingerich-265d7086859.

2. The Dirt, "Kickin' Up The Dirt With Keith Gingerich."

3. Marc Andreessen, "Why Software Is Eating The World," *WSJ*, August 20, 2011, https://www.wsj.com/articles/SB10001424053111903480904576512250915629460?ns=prod/accounts-wsj.

4. Kirk Haney, Interview with author, September 14, 2018.

5. Burwood-Taylor, "What Is Agrifood Tech?"

6. Knud Lasse Lueth, "State of The IoT 2018: Number Of IoT Devices Now At 7B – Market Accelerating," *IoT Analytics*, August 8, 2018, https://iot-analytics.com/state-of-the-iot-update-q1-q2-2018-number-of-iot-devices-now-7b/.

7. "Kickin' Up The Dirt With Keith Gingerich," *The Dirt*, November 11, 2016, https://dirtforfarmers.com/kickin-up-the-dirt-with-keith-gingerich-265d7086859.

8. The Dirt, "Kickin' Up The Dirt With Keith Gingerich."

9. The Dirt, "Kickin' Up The Dirt With Keith Gingerich."

10. "About," Climate Fieldview, accessed February 21, 2019, https://climate.com/about.

11. Julianne Pepitone, "Hacking The Farm: How Farmers Use 'Digital Agriculture' To Grow More Crops," *CNNmoney*, August 3, 2016, https://money.cnn.com/2016/08/03/technology/climate-corporation-digital-agriculture/.

12. Climate Fieldview, "About."

13. Bruce Upbin, "Monsanto Buys Climate Corp For $930 Million," *Forbes*, October 2, 2013, https://www.forbes.com/sites/bruceupbin/2013/10/02/monsanto-buys-climate-corp-for-930-million/#4059d171177a.

14. Upbin, "Monsanto Buys Climate Corp."

15. Pepitone, "Hacking the Farm."

16. "Monsanto To Acquire The Climate Corporation," *Index Ventures*, October 2, 2013, https://www.indexventures.com/news/monsanto-to-acquire-the-climate-corporation.

17. Michael Eaton, Interview with author, August 24, 2018.

18. "Botswana – Agricultural Sectors," Export.gov, last modified July 18, 2017, https://www.export.gov/article?id=Botswana-Agricultural-Sectors.

19. Andrew Maddocks, Robert Samuel Young and Paul Reig, "Ranking The World's Most Water-Stressed Countries In 2040," *World Resources Institute*, August 26, 2015, https://www.wri.org/blog/2015/08/ranking-world-s-most-water-stressed-countries-2040.

20. Remi Schmaltz, "What Is Precision Agriculture And How Is Technology Enabling It?" *AgFunder News*, April 24, 2017, https://agfundernews.com/what-is-precision-agriculture.html.

21. Schmaltz, "What is Precision Agriculture."

22. Jasmeen Nagpal, "Digital Agriculture: Farmers in India Are Using AI To Increase Crop Yields," *Microsoft News Center India*, November 7, 2017, https://news.microsoft.com/en-in/features/ai-agriculture-icrisat-upl-india/.

23. Nagpal, "Digital Agriculture."

24. Nagpal, "Digital Agriculture."

25. Nagpal, "Digital Agriculture."

26. Joseph Shen, Interview with author, October 15, 2018.

27. *Smallholders and Family Farmers*, e-book (Rome: FAO, 2012), http://www.fao.org/fileadmin/templates/nr/sustainability_pathways/docs/Factsheet_SMALLHOLDERS.pdf.

28. "Hunger in India," India FoodBanking Networking, accessed February 21, 2019, https://www.indiafoodbanking.org/hunger.

29. Alec Ross, *Industries of The Future* (New York: Simon & Schuster, 2017), 164-166.

30. Joseph Cotterill, "South Africa: How Cape Town Beat The Drought", *Financial Times*, May 1, 2018, https://www.ft.com/content/b9bac89a-4a49-11e8-8ee8-cae73aab7ccb.

31. "Statistics," Wines of South Africa, accessed February 21, 2019, https://www.wosa.co.za/The-Industry/Statistics/World-Statistics/.

32. Cotterill, "South Africa."

33. Dominique Sian Doyle, Facebook message to author, February 24, 2018.

34. Mahmoud Solh and Maarten van Ginkel, "Drought Preparedness And Drought Mitigation In The Developing World's Drylands," *Weather And Climate Extremes* 3 (2014): 62-66, doi:10.1016/j.wace.2014.03.003.

35. "About," Gro Intelligence, accessed February 21, 2019, https://gro-intelligence.com/about.

36. Gro Intelligence, "About."

37. Barak Cohen, Interview with author, September 7, 2018.

38. World Bank, *High Food Prices: Latin American and Caribbean Responses to a New Normal* (Washington, DC: World Bank, 2014).

39. Conway, *One Billion Hungry*, 7-8.

40. Randolph Barker, Robert Herdt, and Rose Beth. *The Rice Economy of Asia* (Washington, DC: Resources for the Future, 1985).

41. Conway, *One Billion Hungry*, 7-8.

42. "What Are The Facts About Rising Food Prices And Their Effect On The Region?" *World Bank*, September 13, 2012, http://www.worldbank.org/en/news/feature/2012/09/13/america_latina_crisis_precio_alimentos.

43. "Agricultural Market Information System: About," *AMIS*, accessed February 22, 2019, http://www.amis-outlook.org/amis-about/en/.

44. Jaime Adams, "Open Data: Enabling Fact-Based, Data-Driven Decisions," *USDA*, July 13, 2018, https://www.usda.gov/media/blog/2018/07/13/open-data-enabling-fact-based-data-driven-decisions?fbclid=IwAR0K4npGNxv7JblNzdtlhfCIoqSELTchsl7a1l1eopPdrWDYR Kd2plKF9BA.

CHAPTER 2: AGRICULTURAL ROBOTS:
THE DIGITAL FARM WORKER

1. Kelvin Chan, "Robots In The Field: Farms Embracing Autonomous Technology," *PhysOrg*, November 30, 2018, https://phys.org/news/2018-11-robots-field-farms-embracing-autonomous.html.

2. "Small Robot Company," *Small Robot Company*, accessed February 22, 2019, https://www.smallrobotcompany.com/meet-the-robots.

3. Small Robot Company, "Small Robot Company."

4. "U.S. Farmers Encounter Ongoing Farm Labor Shortage," *AgAmerica*, July 12, 2018, https://agamerica.com/farm-labor-shortage/.

5. "Fast Facts About Agriculture," *American Farm Bureau Federation*, accessed February 22, 2019, https://www.fb.org/newsroom/fast-facts.

6. John Newton, "Net Farm Income Projected To Drop To 12-Year Low," *American Farm Bureau Federation*, February 12, 2018, https://www.fb.org/market-intel/net-farm-income-projected-to-drop-to-12-year-low.

7. Newton, "Net Farm Income Projected To Drop To 12-Year Low."

8. Newton, "Net Farm Income Projected To Drop To 12-Year Low."

9. Newton, "Net Farm Income Projected To Drop To 12-Year Low."

10. Johann Tasker, "Farm Labour Shortage 'Worse Than Expected'," *Farmers Weekly UK*, April 26, 2018, https://www.fwi.co.uk/news/eu-referendum/farm-labour-shortage-worse-expected.

11. Jamie Doward and Valentine Baldassari, "Red Alert: UK Farmers Warn Of Soft Fruit Shortage," *The Guardian*, May 27, 2018, https://www.theguardian.com/business/2018/may/27/uk-farmers-strawberries-migrant-workers-crisis.

12. Tasker, "Farm Labour Shortage."

13. Michael Larkin, "Labor Terminators: Farming Robots Are About To Take Over Our Farms," *Investor's Business Daily,* August 10, 2018, https://www.investors.com/news/farming-robot-agriculture-technology/.

14. Gerhard Moitzi et al., "Energy Consumption In Cultivating And Ploughing With Traction Improvement System And Consideration Of The Rear Furrow Wheel-Load In Ploughing," *Soil And Tillage Research* 134 (November 2013): 56-60, doi:10.1016/j.still.2013.07.006.

15. Simon Blackmore, *Dr. Simon Blackmore - Robotic Agriculture: Smarter Machines Using Minimum Energy*, Video, May 11, 2016, https://www.youtube.com/watch?v=4RiWMOz3J4w.

16. Small Robot Company, "Small Robot Company."

17. Ben Scott-Robinson and Sam Watson Jones, Interview with author, October 4, 2018.

18. Tom Simonite, "Why John Deere Just Spent $305 Million On A Lettuce-Farming Robot," *WIRED*, September 6, 2017, https://www.wired.com/story/why-john-deere-just-spent-dollar305-million-on-a-lettuce-farming-robot/.

19. Simonite, "Why John Deere Just Spent $305 Million On A Lettuce-Farming Robot."

20. Louisa Burwood-Taylor, "John Deere Acquires 'See & Spray' Robotics Startup Blue River Technology For $305M," *AgFunder News*, September 6, 2017, https://agfundernews.com/breaking-exclusive-john-deere-acquires-see-spray-robotics-startup-blue-river-technology-305m.html.

21. Simonite, "Why John Deere Just Spent $305 Million On A Lettuce-Farming Robot."

22. "Blue River Technology," *Blue River Technology*, accessed February 23, 2019, http://www.bluerivertechnology.com/.

23. Burwood-Taylor, "John Deere Acquires."

24. Larkin, "Labor Terminators."

25. Larkin, "Labor Terminators."

26. "Agricultural Robots Market By Type & Offering - Global Forecast 2022," *Markets And Markets*, accessed February 23, 2019, https://www.marketsandmarkets.com/Market-Reports/agricultural-robot-market-173601759.html.

27. Burwood-Taylor, "John Deere Acquires."

28. Larkin, "Labor Terminators."

29. Larkin, "Labor Terminators."

30. Ben Scott-Robinson and Sam Watson Jones, Interview with author, October 4, 2018.

31. Small Robot Company, "Small Robot Company."

32. European Agricultural Fund for Rural Development (EAFRD) and Organic Centre Wales, *Why Sustainable Agri-tourism Is A Market Opportunity For The Organic Sector* (Wales: EAFRD, 2011).

33. Kate Baggaley, "Robots Are Replacing Humans In The World's Mines. Here's Why," NBC News, December 21, 2017, https://www.nbcnews.com/mach/science/robots-are-replacing-humans-world-s-mines-here-s-why-ncna831631.

34. Dr. Prabhu Pingali, Interview with author, December 6, 2018.

35. Dr. Prabhu Pingali, Interview with author, December 6, 2018.

CHAPTER 3: DRONES: A FARMER'S EYES IN THE SKY

1. Emma Cosgrove, "American Robotics Raises $2M To Bring Fully Autonomous Drones To Market," *AgFunder News*, February 5, 2018, https://agfundernews.com/american-robotics-raises-second-seed.html.

2. Cosgrove, "American Robotics Raises $2M To Bring Fully Autonomous Drones To Market."

3. FAO (Food and Agriculture Organization of the United Nations) and ITU (International Telecommunication Union), *E-Agriculture In Action: Drones For Agriculture* (Bangkok: FAO and ITU, 2018).

4. FAO and ITU, *E-Agriculture In Action: Drones For Agriculture.*

5. Food and Agriculture Organization of the United Nations and International Telecommunication Union, *E-Agriculture In Action: Drones For Agriculture*.

6. Yeow Chor Lee, Conversation with author, December 4, 2018.

7. "Palms, Palm Oil And Toddies," *Facts And Details*, accessed February 23, 2019, http://factsanddetails.com/world/cat54/sub343/item1576.html.

8. "Plantation," *IOI Group*, accessed February 25, 2019, https://www. ioigroup.com/Content/BUSINESS/B_Plantation.

9. "Global Market For Commercial Applications Of Drone Technology Valued At Over $127 Bn," *Pwc Press Room*, May 9, 2016, https:// press.pwc.com/News-releases/global-market-for-commercial-applications-of-drone-technology-valued-at-over--127-bn/s/ aco4349e-c40d-4767-9f92-a4d219860cd2.

10. FAO and ITU, *E-Agriculture In Action: Drones For Agriculture*.

11. "American Robotics Autonomous Drone System Farming Trials Commence," *American Robotics*, accessed February 23, 2019, http:// www.american-robotics.com/newsblog/2018/8/9/american-robotics-autonomous-drone-system-farming-trials-commence.

12. Jodi Dorman, "As Farmers Grow Drone Use, Privacy Issues Top List Of Concerns," *Business Wire*, July 17, 2018, https:// www.businesswire.com/news/home/20180717005703/en/ Farmers-Grow-Drone-Privacy-Issues-Top-List.

13. FAO and ITU, *E-Agriculture In Action: Drones For Agriculture*.

14. Dorman, "As Farmers Grow Drone Use, Privacy Issues Top List Of Concerns."

15. Scott Elliott, "Global Scientists Meet For Integrated Pest Management Idea Sharing", *NIFA*, April 14, 2015, https://nifa.usda.gov/blog/ global-scientists-meet-integrated-pest-management-idea-sharing.

16. Grand View Research, *Agrochemicals Market Analysis By Product (Fertilizers, Crop Protection Chemicals, Plant Growth Regulators), By Application (Cereals & Grains, Oilseeds & Pulses, Fruits & Vegetables), By Region, And Segment Forecasts, 2018 - 2025* (Grand View Research, Inc, 2017).

17. Jack Roswell and Alex Zhuk, Interview with author, September 13, 2018.

18. David G. Schmale and Shane D. Ross, "Highways In The Sky: Scales Of Atmospheric Transport Of Plant Pathogens," *Annual Review Of Phytopathology* 53, no. 1 (2015): 591-611, doi:10.1146/annurev-phyto-080614-115942.

19. Schmale and Ross, "Highways In The Sky: Scales Of Atmospheric Transport Of Plant Pathogens."

20. Adam Fine, Interview with Author, October 11, 2018.

21. Luke Dormehl, "To Give Bees A Break, Farmers Pollinated An Apple Orchard Using Drones," *Digital Trends*, June 8, 2018, https://www.digitaltrends.com/cool-tech/apple-orchard-pollinated-drones/.

22. "The Role Of The Bee," Greenpeace, accessed February 23, 2019, http://sos-bees.org/situation/.

23. Greenpeace, "The Role of the Bee."

24. Greenpeace, "The Role of the Bee."

25. "Pollinators Vital To Our Food Supply Under Threat," *FAO*, February 26, 2016, http://www.fao.org/news/story/en/item/384726/icode/.

26. Mike H. Allsopp, Willem J. de Lange, and Ruan Veldtman, "Valuing Insect Pollination Services With Cost Of Replacement," *Plos ONE* 3, no. 9 (2008): e3128, doi:10.1371/journal.pone.0003128.

27. "The Economics Of Insect Pollination," *Modern Agriculture*, April 27, 2018, https://modernag.org/biodiversity/beeconomy-economic-value-pollination/.

28. Adam Fine, Interview with Author, October 11, 2018.

29. Adam Fine, Interview with Author, October 11, 2018.

30. FAO, "Pollinators Vital To Our Food Supply Under Threat."

31. "Certificated Remote Pilots Including Commercial Operators," *FAA*, accessed February 23, 2019, https://www.faa.gov/uas/getting_started/part_107/.

32. "Remotely Piloted Aircraft Systems - Frequently Asked Questions," *CASA*, accessed February 23, 2019, https://www.casa.gov.au/aircraft/standard-page/remotely-piloted-aircraft-system-frequently-asked-questions.

33. Maggie Tillman, "Drone Flying In The UK And US: Rules And Regulations Explained," *Pocket-Lint*, January 8, 2019, https://www.pocket-lint.com/drones/news/141667-drone-regulations-and-rules-the-drone-laws-you-need-to-know-before-flying-in-uk-and-us.

34. "How Do We See Them: VLOS, EVLOS, BVLOS & FPV?" *ACUO*, accessed February 23, 2019, http://www.acuo.org.au/industry-information/terminology/how-do-we-see-them/.

35. David Atkinson, "Global Drone Regulations For Hobbyists," *Heliguy*, June 28, 2018, https://www.heliguy.com/blog/2018/06/28/global-drone-regulations-for-hobbyist/.

36. ACUO, "How Do We See Them: VLOS, EVLOS, BVLOS & FPV?"

37. Cosgrove, "American Robotics Raises $2M To Bring Fully Autonomous Drones To Market."

38. Alice Yan, "Over 240 Flights Affected After Drones Disrupt China Airport," *South China Morning Post*, July 20, 2018, https://www.scmp.com/news/china/society/article/2094266/over-240-flights-affected-10000-travellers-stranded-after-drones.

39. Jie Mian, "Drone Regulations In the "Capital of Drones" Shenzhen Wins Applause," *Pandaily,* September 9, 2017, https://pandaily.com/drone-regulations-in-the-capital-of-drones-shenzhen-wins-applause/.

40. Dorman, "As Farmers Grow Drone Use, Privacy Issues Top List Of Concerns."

41. The Dirt, "Kickin' Up The Dirt With Keith Gingerich."

42. Douglas Quinby, "U.S. Private Accommodation Market To Reach $36.6B By 2018," *Phocuswright*, February 2017, https://www.phocuswright.com/Travel-Research/Research-Updates/2017/US-Private-Accommodation-Market-to-Reach-36B-by-2018.

43. Stephen Chen, "How China's Cutting-Edge Drones Are Transforming The Nation," *South China Morning Post*, July 20, 2018, https://www.scmp.com/news/china/society/article/2105798/how-chinas-cutting-edge-drones-are-transforming-nation.

44. Chen, "How China's Cutting-Edge Drones Are Transforming The Nation."

45. "China Population," *Worldometers*, accessed February 25, 2019, http://www.worldometers.info/world-population/china-population/.

46. Chen, "How China's Cutting-Edge Drones Are Transforming The Nation."

47. Chen, "How China's Cutting-Edge Drones Are Transforming The Nation."

48. Chen, "How China's Cutting-Edge Drones Are Transforming The Nation."

49. FAO and ITU, *E-Agriculture In Action: Drones For Agriculture.*

50. FAO and ITU, *E-Agriculture In Action: Drones For Agriculture.*

CHAPTER 4: INDOOR FARMS:
THE ADVENT OF URBAN AGRICULTURE

1. Katie Amey, "Inside The Emirates Catering Factory That Produces 180,000 Meals A Day," *Daily Mail*, January 7, 2016, https://www.dailymail.co.uk/travel/travel_news/article-3387090/1-100-tonnes-lamb-15million-croissants-whopping-91million-tea-bags-Inside-incredible-Emirates-Flight-Catering-Facility-Dubai.html.

2. Chris Dwyer, "Airline Food: How Emirates Airline Can Dish Out 180,000 Meals A Day," *CNN Travel*, March 16, 2017, https://edition.cnn.com/travel/article/emirates-flight-catering/index.html.

3. Dwyer, "Airline Food: How Emirates Airline Can Dish Out 180,000 Meals A Day."

4. Kim Tormey, "Emirates Flight Catering Builds World'S Largest Vertical Farming Facility In Dubai," *Emirates Flight Catering*, June 26, 2018, https://www.emiratesflightcatering.com/about-us/news-press/emirates-flight-catering-builds-world-s-largest-vertical-farming-facility-in-dubai/.

5. Tormey, "Emirates Flight Catering Builds World'S Largest Vertical Farming Facility In Dubai."

6. Vera Colstee, "The History Of Indoor Vertical Farming," *EIT Food*, accessed February 23, 2019, https://www.eitfood.eu/blog/post/the-origins-of-indoor-vertical-farming.

7. Colstee, "The History Of Indoor Vertical Farming."

8. Ian Frazier, "The Vertical Farm," *The New Yorker*, January 9, 2017, https://www.newyorker.com/magazine/2017/01/09/the-vertical-farm.

9. Frazier, "The Vertical Farm."

10. Lora Kolodny and Magdalena Petrova, "Bowery Farming Is Growing Crops In Warehouses To Create Food Like Customized Kale," *CNBC*, May 24, 2018, https://www.cnbc.com/2018/05/24/bowery-farming-growing-crops-in-warehouses.html.

11. "Cornell Controlled Environment Agriculture: About Cornell CEA," *Cornell CALS*, accessed February 23, 2019, http://cea.cals.cornell.edu/about/index.html.

12. Oliver Balch, "This Swedish Indoor Urban Farm Wants To Revolutionize Growing Food In Cities," *Huffpost*, April 4, 2018, https://www.huffingtonpost.com/entry/plantagon-urban-farm-sweden_us_5a9698cfe4b0e6a523033b7c.

13. Jeff Edwards, "Hydroponics History Part 2 | The Birth Of Hydroponics," *Hydroponics*, accessed February 23, 2019, http://hydroponicgardening.com/history-of-hydroponics/the-birth-of-hydroponics/.

14. Edwards, "Hydroponics History Part 2 | The Birth Of Hydroponics."

15. Frank J. Taylor, *The Rotarian* (Cleveland: Rotary International, 1939), 14-15.

16. Taylor, *The Rotarian*, 14-15.

17. Taylor, *The Rotarian*, 14-15.

18. Bambi Turner, "How Hydroponics Works," *How Stuff Works*, accessed February 23, 2019, https://home.howstuffworks.com/lawn-garden/professional-landscaping/hydroponics1.htm.

19. "Hydroponics: Forecasted Market Value Worldwide 2016-2025," *Statista*, accessed February 23, 2019, https://www.statista.com/statistics/879946/global-hydroponics-market-value/.

20. "Global Hydroponics Market To Reach Valuation Of US$12.1 Bn By 2025; Vertical Cultivation To Offer New Opportunities For Market Players - Transparency Market Research," *PR Newswire*, July 10. 2018, https://www.prnewswire.com/news-releases/global-hydroponics-market-to-reach-valuation-of-us-12-1-bn-by-2025-vertical-cultivation-to-offer-new-opportunities-for-market-players-transparency-market-research-870167916.html.

21. Taylor, *The Rotarian*, 14-15.

22. "5 Hydroponic Fun Facts And Figures," *Visually*, accessed February 23, 2019, https://visual.ly/community/infographic/environment/5-hydroponic-fun-facts-and-figures.

23. Aimee Lutkin, "The Future Of Farming Is Moving Indoors. Here's Why," *World Economic Forum*, March 7, 2018, https://www.weforum.org/agenda/2018/03/this-indoor-farm-is-trying-to-revolutionize-the-growing-process-in-sweden.

24. FAO, *Integrated Agriculture-aquaculture: A Primer* (Rome: FAO, 2001), 68-69.

25. Amelia Pang, "New York City Might Be Able To Mass Produce Its Own Food With Aquaponics," *The Epoch Times*, March 7, 2015, https://www.theepochtimes.com/new-york-city-might-be-able-to-mass-produce-its-own-food-with-aquaponics_1273946.html.

26. "Aquaponics As A Way To Reduce Food Imports In The Caribbean," *Hortidaily*, August 14, 2018, https://www.hortidaily.com/article/6045090/aquaponics-as-a-way-to-reduce-food-imports-in-the-caribbean/.

27. Sylvia Bernstein, "The Way Of The Future: Aquaponics Vs. Traditional Agriculture," *Innerself*, accessed February 23, 2019, https://innerself.com/content/living/home-and-garden/gardening/8654-aquaponics-vs-traditional-agriculture.html.

28. Cathy Siegner, "Brightfarms Building $17M Hydroponic Greenhouse In Texas," *Food Dive*, March 23, 2018, https://www.fooddive.com/news/brightfarms-building-17m-hydroponic-greenhouse-in-texas/519892/.

29. Siegner, "Brightfarms Building $17M Hydroponic Greenhouse In Texas."

30. Mark Perelman, "Vertical Farming Climbs In Cleveland, Chicago, New York," *Greenbiz*, November 22, 2017, https://www.greenbiz.com/article/vertical-farming-climbs-cleveland-chicago-new-york.

31. Thin Lei Win, "Urban Farm 'Critical' To Combat Hunger and Adapt To Climate Change," *Thomson Reuters News,* January 11, 2018, http://news.trust.org/item/20180111102522-tb51m/.

32. Win, "Urban Farm."

33. Win, "Urban Farm."

34. Stacey Shackford, "Indoor Urban Farms Called Wasteful, 'Pie In The Sky'," *Cornell Chronicle*, February 19, 2014, http://news.cornell.edu/stories/2014/02/indoor-urban-farms-called-wasteful-pie-sky.

35. "Cost Of Living In The United States," *Study in US*, accessed February 23, 2019, http://www.studying-in-us.org/cost-of-living-in-the-united-states/.

36. Patrick Caughill, "Urban Farming Is The Future of Agriculture," *Futurism,* January 16, 2018, https://futurism.com/urban-farming-future-agriculture.

37. Shackford, "Indoor Urban Farms Called Wasteful, 'Pie In The Sky'."

38. Aimee Lutkin, "The Future Of Farming Is Moving Indoors. Here's Why."

39. Aimee Lutkin, "The Future Of Farming Is Moving Indoors. Here's Why."

40. Aimee Lutkin, "The Future Of Farming Is Moving Indoors. Here's Why."

41. Caughill, "Urban Farming Is The Future Of Agriculture."

42. Caughill, "Urban Farming Is The Future Of Agriculture."

43. Viviano, "This Tiny Country Feed the World."

44. Viviano, "This Tiny Country Feed the World."

45. Viviano, "This Tiny Country Feed the World."

46. "Israel's Chronic Water Problem," *Israel Ministry of Foreign Affairs,* accessed February 25, 2019, https://mfa.gov.il/MFA/IsraelExperience/AboutIsrael/Spotlight/Pages/Israel-s%20Chronic%20Water%20Problem.aspx.

47. "Uganda Can Pick Better Agric Lessons From Israel," *New Vision*, March 13, 2017, https://www.newvision.co.ug/new_vision/news/1448404/uganda-pick-agric-lessons-israel.

48. "Vermiculite in Hydroponics," *Palabora Europe,* last accessed February 25, 2019, https://palaboraeurope.co.uk/vermiculite-in-hydroponics/.

49. "Agriculture Land (% of land area)," *The World Bank*, accessed February 23, 2019, https://data.worldbank.org/indicator/AG.LND.AGRI.ZS?locations=SG.

50. Cecilia Tortajada and Thinesh Kumar, "Singapore's Impressive Food Security," *The Diplomat*, September 6, 2015, https://thediplomat. com/2015/09/singapores-impressive-food-security/.

51. Natasha Zachariah, "Urban Farming In Singapore Has Moved Into A New, High-Tech Phase," *The Straits Times*, June 3, 2017, https://www. straitstimes.com/lifestyle/home-design/fresh-ideas-for-city-farms.

52. Darren Ho, Interview with author, September 14, 2018.

53. The World Bank, "Agricultural Land (% Of Land Area)."

54. Elan Perumal, "MB: Selangor Will Maintain Land For Farming - Metro News," *The Star Online*, August 10, 2018, https://www.thestar.com.my/metro/metro-news/2018/08/10/ mb-selangor-will-maintain-land-for-farming/.

55. Meghan Horvath, "Making Sense Of The Terms In Vertical Farming," *EIT Food*, accessed February 23, 2019, https://www.eitfood.eu/blog/ post/making-sense-of-the-terms-in-vertical-farming.

CHAPTER 5: SMART MICRO-GARDENS:
THE DEMOCRATIZATION OF FOOD PRODUCTION

1. "System — SproutsIO," *SproutsIO*, accessed February 23, 2019, https:// www.sprouts.io/system/.

2. Kris Naudus, "The Sproutsio Smart Microgarden Nurtures Your Inner Botanist," *Engadget*, September 21, 2016, https://www.engadget. com/2016/09/21/sproutsio-smart-microgarden/.

3. Erika Velazquez, "Oligopoly: Breakfast Cereals Industry," (Presentation, December 1, 2014).

4. "Mega-Mergers In The Global Agricultural Inputs Sector: Threats To Food Security & Climate Resilience," (Presentation, September 2015).

5. John Vidal, "Farming Mega-Mergers Threaten Food Security, Say Campaigners," *The Guardian*, September 26, 2016, https:// www.theguardian.com/global-development/2016/sep/26/ farming-mega-mergers-threaten-food-security-say-campaigners.

6. Vidal, "Farming Mega-Mergers Threaten Food Security, Say Campaigners."

7. Vidal, "Farming Mega-Mergers Threaten Food Security, Say Campaigners."

8. Vidal, "Farming Mega-Mergers Threaten Food Security, Say Campaigners."

9. Vidal, "Farming Mega-Mergers Threaten Food Security, Say Campaigners."

10. Craig Giammona, "Big Food'S Deal Frenzy Is Just Getting Started," *Bloomberg*, December 19, 2017, https://www.bloomberg.com/news/articles/2017-12-19/boom-in-food-m-a-deals-is-just-getting-started-as-kraft-looms.

11. "Food Sovereignty," *USFSA*, accessed February 23, 2019, http://usfoodsovereigntyalliance.org/what-is-food-sovereignty/.

12. "SproutsIO Smart Microgarden (Presale)," *SproutsIO*, accessed February 23, 2019, https://shop.sprouts.io/sproutsio-presale/.

13. "Ecogarden: World's Smartest Interactive Ecosystem," *Indiegogo*, accessed February 23, 2019, https://www.indiegogo.com/projects/ecogarden-world-s-smartest-interactive-ecosystem#/.

14. John Callaham, "Amazon Echo Is Now Available For Everyone To Buy For $179.99, Shipments Start On July 14," *Android Central*, June 23, 2015, https://www.androidcentral.com/amazon-echo-now-available-everyone-buy-17999-shipments-start-july-14.

15. "Echo (2nd Generation) - Smart Speaker With Alexa - Charcoal Fabric," *Amazon*, accessed February 23, 2019, https://www.amazon.com/all-new-amazon-echo-speaker-with-wifi-alexa-dark-charcoal/dp/B06XCM9LJ4/ref=asc_df_B06XCM9LJ4/?tag=hyprod-20&linkCode=df0&hvadid=198057002855&hvpos=1o1&hvnetw=g&hvrand=6396713076217081950&hvpone=&hvptwo=&hvqmt=&hvdev=c&hvdvcmdl=&hvlocint=&hvlocphy=1023037&hvtargid=pla-370806212301&psc=1.

16. "IKEA Launches Indoor Garden That Can Grow Food All Year-Round," *Inhabitant*, March 19. 2016, https://inhabitat.com/ikea-launches-indoor-garden-that-can-grow-food-all-year-round/.

CHAPTER 6: GMOS: THE FORBIDDEN HERO

1. Michael Hoffman, Interview with author, September 7, 2018.

2. Richard Fama, "The New GMO Labeling Law: A Matter Of Perspective," *Food Safety News*, September 8, 2016, https://www.foodsafetynews.com/2016/09/the-new-gmo-labeling-law-a-matter-of-perspective/.

3. "Climate Impacts On Agriculture And Food Supply," *EPA*, accessed February 23, 2019, https://19january2017snapshot.epa.gov/climate-impacts/climate-impacts-agriculture-and-food-supply_.html#ref1.

4. "Global Warming: More Insects, Eating More Crops," *PhysOrg*, August 30, 2018, https://phys.org/news/2018-08-global-insects-crops.html.

5. PhysOrg, "Global Warming: More Insects, Eating More Crops."

6. "How Does GM Differ From Conventional Plant Breeding? | Royal Society," *The Royal Society*, accessed February 23, 2019, https://royalsociety.org/topics-policy/projects/gm-plants/how-does-gm-differ-from-conventional-plant-breeding/.

7. "Conventional Plant Breeding," *ISAAA*, accessed February 23, 2019, http://www.isaaa.org/resources/publications/pocketk/13/default.asp.

8. David A. Jackson, Robert H. Symons and Paul Berg, "Biochemical Method For Inserting New Genetic Information Into DNA Of Simian Virus 40: Circular SV40 DNA Molecules Containing Lambda Phage Genes And The Galactose Operon Of Escherichia Coli," *PNAS* 69, no. 10 (October 1972).

9. "Codex Alimentarius International Food Standards," FAO, accessed February 25, 2019, http://www.fao.org/fao-who-codexalimentarius/en/.

10. "The Nature of GMOs," *FAO*, accessed February 23, 2019, http://www.fao.org/3/Y4955E/y4955e03.htm#TopOfPage.

11. FAO, "The Nature of GMOs."

12. "Genetically Modified Organisms: The "Golden Rice" Debate," *NYU Langone Health*, accessed February 23, 2019, https://med.nyu.edu/highschoolbioethics/genetically-modified-organisms-%E2%80%9Cgolden-rice%E2%80%9D-debate.

13. Jan Nyrop, Interview with author, September 21, 2018.

14. "Micronutrient Deficiencies," *WHO*, accessed February 23, 2019, https://www.who.int/nutrition/topics/vad/en/.

15. Julianna LeMieux, "What Is CRISPR-Cas9 And Why Do We Need To Know About It?" *American Council On Science And Health*, May 25, 2016, https://www.acsh.org/news/2016/05/25/what-is-crispr-cas9-and-why-do-we-need-to-know-about-it

16. NYU Langone Health, "Genetically Modified Organisms: The "Golden Rice" Debate."

17. Jan Nyrop, Interview with author, September 21, 2018.

18. Oliver Balch, "Are Drought-Resistant Crops In Africa The Tech Fix They're Cracked Up To Be?" *The Guardian*, September 2, 2016, https://www.theguardian.com/sustainable-business/2016/sep/02/drought-resistant-crops-gm-africa-monsanto-syngenta-dupont.

19. FAO, *The State Of Agricultural Commodity Markets 2018* (Rome: FAO, 2018).

20. Wilhelm Klümper and Matin Qaim, "A Meta-Analysis Of The Impacts Of Genetically Modified Crops," *Plos ONE* 9, no. 11 (2014): e111629, doi:10.1371/journal.pone.0111629.

21. David Rotman, "GMOs Could Be An Important Tool In Feeding The World," *MIT Technology Review*, December 17, 2013, https://www.technologyreview.com/s/522596/why-we-will-need-genetically-modified-foods/.

22. Mark Lynas, "Confession Of An Anti-GMO Activist," *WSJ*, June 22, 2018, https://www.wsj.com/articles/confession-of-an-anti-gmo-activist-1529679465?ns=prod/accounts-wsj.

23. Mark Lynas, *Seeds Of Science Why We Got It So Wrong On GMOs*, ebook, 1st ed. (Bloomsbury Sigma, May 4, 2018), https://www.bloomsbury.com/uk/seeds-of-science-9781472946959/.

24. Lynas, "Confession Of An Anti-GMO Activist."

25. Lynas, "Confession Of An Anti-GMO Activist."

26. "Genetically Engineered Crops," *National Academies Of Sciences, Engineering, And Medicine*, 2016, doi:https://doi.org/10.17226/23395.

27. Jennifer A. Doudna, "A Crack In Creation Quotes," *Goodreads*, accessed February 23, 2019, https://www.goodreads.com/work/quotes/51589493-a-crack-in-creation-gene-editing-and-the-unthinkable-power-to-control-e.

28. Jane E. Brody, "Are G.M.O. Foods Safe?" *The New York Times*, April 23, 2018, https://www.nytimes.com/2018/04/23/well/eat/are-gmo-foods-safe.html.

29. Michael Hoffman, Interview with author, September 7, 2018.

30. Lessley Anderson, "Why Does Everyone Hate Monsanto?" *Modern Farmer*, March 4, 2014, https://modernfarmer.com/2014/03/monsantos-good-bad-pr-problem/.

31. Lynas, "Confession Of An Anti-GMO Activist."

32. Steven Cerier, "Genetic Engineering, CRISPR And Food: What The 'Revolution' Will Bring In The Near Future," *Genetic Literacy Project*, January 24, 2018, https://geneticliteracyproject.org/2018/01/24/genetic-engineering-crispr-food-revolution-will-bring-near-future/.

33. Gabriel Miller, "Medical Breakthroughs That Were Initially Ridiculed Or Rejected," *Medscape*, November 19, 2015, https://www.medscape.com/features/slideshow/medical-breakthroughs.

34. Stephen O. Duke, "Glyphosate-Resistant Crops And Weeds: Now And In The Future," *Agbioforum* 12, no. 3 & 4 (2009): 346-357, http://www.agbioforum.org/v12n34/v12n34a10-duke.htm.

35. Mary Ellen Kustin, "Glyphosate Is Spreading Like A Cancer Across The U.S." *Agmag*, April 7. 2015, https://www.ewg.org/agmag/2015/04/glyphosate-spreading-cancer-across-us.

36. Klümper and Qaim, "A Meta-Analysis Of The Impacts Of Genetically Modified Crops."

37. Lynas, "Confession Of An Anti-GMO Activist."

CHAPTER 7: CRISPR: THE FRONTIER OF GENE EDITING

1. Roger Rossignol, "Bananas World's Most Popular Fruit. - A Passion For Food," *Westcountry*, May 25, 2017, http://www.apassionforfood.co.uk/bananas/.

2. "Banana Facts And Figures," *FAO*, accessed February 23, 2019, http://www.fao.org/economic/est/est-commodities/bananas/bananafacts/en/#.XHFzhehKguH.

3. Matt Reynolds, "The Banana Is Dying. The Race Is On To Reinvent It Before It's Too Late," *Wired*, OCtober 11, 2018, https://www.wired.co.uk/article/cavendish-banana-extinction-gene-editing.

4. Reynolds, "The Banana Is Dying."

5. Reynolds, "The Banana Is Dying."

6. Reynolds, "The Banana Is Dying."

7. Reynolds, "The Banana Is Dying."

8. Daniel Workman, "Bananas Exports By Country," *World's Top Exports*, January 15, 2019, http://www.worldstopexports.com/bananas-exports-country/.

9. Cerier, "Genetic Engineering, CRISPR And Food: What The 'Revolution' Will Bring In The Near Future."

10. Reynolds, "The Banana Is Dying."

11. Yi Li, "These CRISPR-Modified Crops Don't Count As GMOs," *The Conversation*, May 22, 2018, https://theconversation.com/these-crispr-modified-crops-dont-count-as-gmos-96002.

12. Deborah Netburn, "New Genome Editing Technique Can Target Single Letters Of DNA Sequence," *Los Angeles Times*, April 21, 2016, https://www.latimes.com/science/sciencenow/la-sci-sn-a-crispr-base-editing-20160420-story.html

13. "Questions and Answers About CRISPR," *Broad Institute,* accessed January 25, 2019, https://www.broadinstitute.org/what-broad/areas-focus/project-spotlight/questions-and-answers-about-crispr.

14. Netburn, "New Genome Editing Technique Can Target Single Letters Of DNA Sequence."

15. LeMieux, "What Is CRISPR-Cas9."

16. Mohammad Miransari, *Environmental Stress Conditions in Soybean Production: Soybean Production, Volume Two* (Academic Press, 2016), 131-156.

17. Keith Speights, "CRISPR Therapeutics Stock History: The Rise Of The World's Biggest Gene-Editing Biotech," *The Motley Fool*, July 16, 2018, https://www.fool.com/investing/2018/07/16/crispr-therapeutics-stock-history-the-rise-of-the.aspx.

18. Speights, "CRISPR Therapeutics Stock History: The Rise Of The World's Biggest Gene-Editing Biotech."

19. Brad Plumer et al., "A Simple Guide To CRISPR, One Of The Biggest Science Stories Of The Decade," *Vox*, December 27, 2018, https://www.vox.com/2018/7/23/17594864/crispr-cas9-gene-editing.

20. Plumer et al., "A Simple Guide To CRISPR, One Of The Biggest Science Stories Of The Decade."

21. FAO, "The Nature of GMOs."

22. Emily Waltz, "Gene-Edited CRISPR Mushroom Escapes US Regulation," *Nature* 532, no. 7599 (2016): 293-293, doi:10.1038/nature.2016.19754.

23. Waltz, "Gene-Edited CRISPR Mushroom."

24. Li, "These CRISPR-Modified Crops Don't Count As GMOs."

25. Li, "These CRISPR-Modified Crops Don't Count As GMOs."

26. "Joyce Van Eck," *Genome Editing Symposium*, accessed February 23, 2019, https://genome-editing-symposium-tamu.com/joyce-van-eck/.

27. Joyce Van Eck, Interview with author, October 23, 3018.

28. Joyce Van Eck, Interview with author, October 23, 3018.

29. Joyce Van Eck, Interview with author, October 23, 3018.

30. Mike Carroll, "CRISPR Tames The Wild Groundcherry," *Boyce Thompson Institute*, October 1, 2018, https://btiscience.org/explore-bti/news/post/crispr-tames-the-wild-groundcherry/.

31. "Food For All - World Food Summit - Agricultural Machinery Worldwide," *FAO*, accessed February 23, 2019, http://www.fao.org/3/x0262e/x0262e02.htm.

32. "Dimensions Of Need - Staple Foods: What Do People Eat?" *FAO*, accessed February 23, 2019, http://www.fao.org/3/u8480e/u8480e07.htm.

33. "Seeds Of Life," *FAO*, accessed February 23, 2019, http://www.fao.org/3/x0262e/x0262e02.htm.

34. FAO, "Seeds Of Life."

35. "Irish Potato Famine," *History*, accessed February 23, 2019, https://www.history.com/topics/immigration/irish-potato-famine.

36. History, ""Irish Potato Famine."

37. Waltz, "Gene-Edited CRISPR Mushroom Escapes US Regulation."

38. "Emerging Techniques In Biotechnology Pose New Risks To The Non-GMO Supply Chain – The Non-GMO Project," *Non GMO Project*, August 2, 2018, https://www.nongmoproject.org/blog/emerging-techniques-in-biotechnology-pose-new-risks-to-the-non-gmo-supply-chain/.

39. Ewen Callaway, "CRISPR Plants Now Subject To Tough GM Laws In European Union," *Nature*, July 25, 2018, https://www.nature.com/articles/d41586-018-05814-6.

40. Cerier, "Genetic Engineering, CRISPR And Food: What The 'Revolution' Will Bring In The Near Future."

CHAPTER 8: A BETTER WAY TO (M)EAT

1. Paul Shapiro, "Commentary: Can Lab-Grown Meat Feed—And Save—The World?" *Reuters*, February 26, 2018, https://www.reuters.com/article/us-shapiro-meat-commentary/commentary-science-fiction-no-more-can-lab-grown-meat-feed-and-save-the-world-idUSKCN1GA25H.

2. Vaclav Smil, "Eating Meat: Evolution, Patterns, And Consequences," *Population And Development Review* 28, no. 4 (December 2002): 599-639, http://home.cc.umanitoba.ca/~vsmil/pdf_pubs/PDR2003.pdf.

3. Smil, "Eating Meat: Evolution, Patterns, And Consequences."

4. "What Is Cultured Meat?" *New Harvest*, accessed February 23, 2019, https://www.new-harvest.org/what_is_cultured_meat.

5. J. Poore and T. Nemecek, "Reducing Food'S Environmental Impacts Through Producers And Consumers," *Science* 360, no. 6392 (June 2018): 987-992, doi:10.1126/science.aaq0216.

6. Poore and Nemecek, "Reducing Food'S Environmental Impacts Through Producers And Consumers."

7. Arjen Y. Hoekstra, "The Hidden Water Resource Use Behind Meat And Dairy," *Animal Frontiers* 2, no. 2 (April 2011): 3-8, doi:https://doi.org/10.2527/af.2012-0038.

8. "Home," *Water Footprint*, accessed February 23, 2019, https://waterfootprint.org/en/.

9. "Water Stress To Affect 52% Of world's Population By 2050," *Water Footprint*, accessed February 23, 2019, https://waterfootprint.org/en/about-us/news/news/water-stress-affect-52-worlds-population-2050/.

10. CB Insights, "Memphis Meats," available via CB Insights, accessed February 25, 2019,

11. "Just, Inc," *Crunchbase*, accessed February 24, 2019, https://www.crunchbase.com/organization/just-inc#section-overview.

12. "Forecast Processed Meat Market Value Worldwide 2016-2022," *Statista*, accessed February 24, 2019, https://www.statista.com/statistics/911596/forecast-global-market-value-of-processed-meat/

13. "Yes, This Is Actual Meat, But No Animal Died For It," *PETA*, March 21, 2017, https://www.peta.org/living/food/memphis-meats-debuts-lab-grown-chicken-clean-meat/.

14. Emily Byrd, "Meet GFI Innovation Specialist Aylon Steinhart!" *The Good Food Institute*, February 19, 2018, https://www.gfi.org/2018-02-19.

15. Aylon Steinhart, interview with author, September 12, 2018.

16. Aylon Steinhart, interview with author, September 12, 2018.

17. Bruce Friedrich, ""Clean Meat": The "Clean Energy" Of Food," *The Good Food Institute*, September 6, 2016, https://www.gfi.org/clean-meat-the-clean-energy-of-food.

18. Friedrich, ""Clean Meat": The "Clean Energy" Of Food."

19. "5 Reasons Why You Should Avoid Store Made Ground Meat And Why You Should Ground Your Own!" *The Hamptons Butcher*, March 30, 2018, http://thehamptonsbutcher.com/index.php/2018/03/30/5-reasons-why-you-should-avoid-store-made-ground-meat-and-why-you-should-grind-your-own/.

20. Matti Wilks and Clive J. C. Phillips, "Attitudes To In Vitro Meat: A Survey Of Potential Consumers In The United States," *PLOS ONE* 12, no. 2 (February 16, 2017): e0171904, doi:10.1371/journal.pone.0171904.

21. Maddie Stone, "The Future Will Be Full Of Lab Grown Meat," *Gizmodo*, May 27, 2018, https://gizmodo.com/the-future-will-be-full-of-lab-grown-meat-1720874704.

22. Jacob Bunge, "Startup Producing Cell-Grown Meat Raises New Funding," *WSJ*, July 16, 2018, https://www.wsj.com/articles/startup-producing-cell-grown-meat-raises-new-funding-1531738800?mod=e2fb&ns=prod/accounts-wsj.

23. "Memphis Meats: We'll Have 'Clean Meat' Products In Grocery Stores By 2021," *Food Navigator*, accessed February 24, 2019, https://www.foodnavigator-usa.com/Article/2016/12/02/We-ll-have-clean-meat-in-grocery-stores-by-2021-Memphis-Meats.

24. Foodnavigator, "Memphis Meats: We'll Have 'Clean Meat' Products In Grocery Stores By 2021."

25. Matt Reynolds, "The Clean Meat Industry Is Racing To Ditch Its Reliance On Foetal Blood," *WIRED*, March 20, 2018, https://www.wired.co.uk/article/scaling-clean-meat-serum-just-finless-foods-mosa-meat.

26. Reynolds, "The Clean Meat Industry Is Racing."

27. Reynolds, "The Clean Meat Industry Is Racing."

28. Reynolds, "The Clean Meat Industry Is Racing."

29. Aylon Steinhart, interview with author, September 12, 2018.

30. Chloe Sorvino, "Tyson Invests In Lab-Grown Protein Startup Memphis Meats, Joining Bill Gates And Richard Branson," *Forbes*, January 29, 2018, https://www.forbes.com/sites/chloesorvino/2018/01/29/exclusive-interview-tyson-invests-in-lab-grown-protein-startup-memphis-meats-joining-bill-gates-and-richard-branson/#261da0793351.

31. Sorvino, "Tyson Invests In Lab-Grown Protein Startup Memphis Meats, Joining Bill Gates And Richard Branson."

32. Food Navigator, "Memphis Meats: We'll Have 'Clean Meat' Products In Grocery Stores By 2021."

33. Charlotte Hawks, "How Close Are We To A Hamburger Grown In A Lab?" *CNN*, March 8. 2018, https://www.cnn.com/2018/03/01/health/clean-in-vitro-meat-food/index.html.

34. "No Conclusion On Cell-Cultured Animal Products At USDA-FDA Meeting," *The Fence Post*, October 25, 2018, https://www.thefencepost.com/news/no-conclusion-on-cell-cultured-animal-products-at-usda-fda-meeting/.

35. The Fence Post, "No Conclusion On Cell-Cultured Animal Products At USDA-FDA Meeting."

36. Hawks, "How Close Are We To A Hamburger Grown In A Lab?"

37. Friedrich, ""Clean Meat": The "Clean Energy" Of Food."

38. The Fence Post, "No Conclusion On Cell-Cultured Animal Products At USDA-FDA Meeting."

39. Sam Bloch, "Dispatch From D.C.: USDA And FDA Agree To Jointly Regulate Cell-Cultured Meat. And Yes, It's Meat," *New Food Economy*, OCtober 25, 2018, https://newfoodeconomy.org/usda-fda-lab-grown-cell-cultured-joint-regulation/.

40. Jill Ettinger, "Vegan Beyond Burger Outsells Beef In Major Supermarket's Meat Case," *LIVEKINDLY*, March 8, 2018, https://www.livekindly.co/vegan-beyond-burger-outsells-beef-at-major-supermarkets-meat-case/.

41. Maria Chiorando, "Beyond Meat To Double Production As It Outsells Beef In Some Stores," *Plant Based News*, June 6, 2018, https://www.plantbasednews.org/post/beyond-meat-to-double-production-outsells-beef.

42. Leanna Garfield, "The Bill Gates-Backed Veggie Burger That 'Bleeds' Like Beef Is Coming To America's Largest Grocery Chain — Here's What It Tastes Like," *Business Insider*, July 27, 2017, https://www.businessinsider.com/review-beyond-meat-veggie-burger-bill-gates-2017-7.

43. "Forecast Processed Meat Market Value Worldwide 2016-2022," *Statista*, accessed February 24, 2019, https://www.statista.com/statistics/911596/forecast-global-market-value-of-processed-meat/.

44. Laura Wood, "Meat Substitutes - Worldwide Market Outlook To 2023: Analysis By Type, Source, Category And Region - High Growth Potential In The Asia-Pacific Market," *Business Wire*, July 2, 2018, https://www.businesswire.com/news/home/20180702005609/en/Meat-Substitutes---Worldwide-Market-Outlook-2023.

45. Elaine Watson, "US Retail Sales Of Plant-Based Milk Up 9%, Plant-Based Meat Up 24% YoY," *Food Navigator USA*, July 30, 2018, https://www.foodnavigator-usa.com/Article/2018/07/30/US-retail-sales-of-plant-based-milk-up-9-plant-based-meat-up-24-YoY.

46. Bill Gates, "Future of Food," *Gates Notes,* March 18, 2013, https://www.gatesnotes.com/About-Bill-Gates/Future-of-Food.

47. Mary Ellen Shoup, "Beyond Meat Secures Non-GMO Status, On Quest 'To Be On The Center Of The Plate For The Entire Family'," *Food Navigator USA*, July 23, 2018, https://www.foodnavigator-usa.com/Article/2018/07/23/Beyond-Meat-secures-non-GMO-status.

48. Jessica Appelgren, "Impossible Foods' 2018 Impact Report Details The Food Tech Startup'S Strategic Roadmap," *Business Wire*, August 8, 2018, https://www.businesswire.com/news/home/20180808005236/en/Impossible-Foods%E2%80%99-2018-Impact-Report-Details-Food.

49. Personal conversation with grill cook at Trillium Cafe, December 2, 2018.

50. Murali Saravanan, "Making The Impossible Possible," *The Cornell Daily Sun*, March 28, 2018, https://cornellsun.com/2018/03/28/making-the-impossible-possible/.

51. Saravanan, "Making The Impossible Possible."

52. Martin C. Heller and Gregory A. Keoleian, *Beyond Meat'S Beyond Burger Life Cycle Assessment: A Detailed Comparison Between A Plantbased And An Animal-Based Protein Source*, Beyond Burger LCA Report (Michigan: Regents of the University of Michigan, September 14, 2018), http://css.umich.edu/sites/default/files/publication/CSS18-10.pdf.

53. Katrina Fox, "This Vegan Brand Just Proved That Plant-Based Burgers Are More Sustainable Than Those Made Of Beef," *Forbes*, September 26, 2018, https://www.forbes.com/sites/katrinafox/2018/09/26/this-vegan-brand-just-proved-that-plant-based-burgers-are-more-sustainable-than-those-made-of-beef/?utm_source=FBPAGE&utm_medium=social&utm_content=1804185560&utm_campaign=sprinklrForbesMainFB#13707c65475a.

54. "Plant-Based Proteins Are Gaining Dollar Share Among North Americans," *Neilsen*, September 22, 2017, https://www.nielsen.com/us/en/insights/news/2017/plant-based-proteins-are-gaining-dollar-share-among-north-americans.html.

55. Nielsen, "Plant-Based Proteins Are Gaining Dollar Share Among North Americans."

56. Ellie Anzilotti, "Impossible Foods Is Making 500,000 Pounds Of Fake Meat A Month," *Fast Company*, August 8, 2018, https://www.fastcompany.com/90214790/impossible-foods-is-making-500000-pounds-of-fake-meat-a-month.

57. Chiorando, "Beyond Meat To Double Production As It Outsells Beef In Some Stores."

58. Watson, "US Retail Sales Of Plant-Based Milk Up 9%, Plant-Based Meat Up 24% YoY."

59. U.S. Senate, *SENATE BILLS NOS. 627 & 925* (U.S. Senate, 2018).

60. Lucia Binding, "France Bans Meat Related Words From Vegetarian Food Packets," *Evening Standard*, April 25, 2018, https://www.standard.co.uk/news/world/france-bans-meat-and-dairy-related-words-from-vegetarian-and-vegan-food-packets-a3822831.html.

61. Erin Brodwin, "The Startup Behind Silicon Valley'S Favorite 'Bleeding' Veggie Burger Has Scored A Major Victory In Its Battle For Legitimacy," *Business Insider*, July 23, 2018, https://www.businessinsider.com/impossible-foods-bleeding-veggie-burger-ingredient-gets-fda-green-light-2018-7.

62. "US Non-Dairy Milk Sales Grow 61% Over The Last 5 Years," *Mintel*, January 4, 2018, http://www.mintel.com/press-centre/food-and-drink/us-non-dairy-milk-sales-grow-61-over-the-last-five-years.

63. Madeline Stone, "How A Startup That Makes Fake Meat From Plants Caught The Attention Of Bill Gates And The Founders Of Twitter," *Business Insider,* August 15, 2015, https://www.businessinsider.com/how-a-startup-that-makes-fake-meat-from-plants-caught-the-attention-of-bill-gates-and-the-founders-of-twitter-2015-7.

64. Kat Smith, "Largest Meat Producer In the U.S. To Launch Vegan Protein," *LIVEKINDLY,* February 11, 2019, https://www.livekindly.co/largest-meat-producer-us-vegan-protein/.

CHAPTER 9: FOOD WASTE TECHNOLOGY

1. Chris Huber, "World's Food Waste Could Feed 2 Billion People," *World Vision*, accessed February 24, 2019, https://www.worldvision.org/hunger-news-stories/food-waste.

2. "Cornell Dining Leaps To Its Highest Spot Ever In Princeton Review's Campus Food Ranking," *Living At Cornell*, August 30, 2016, https://living.cornell.edu/explore/news/1608-dining-princeton-review.cfm.

3. Tanja Srebotnjak, "Food Waste At U.S. Colleges And What To Do About It," *Huffpost*, August 23, 2016, https://www.huffingtonpost.com/entry/food-waste-at-us-colleges-and-what-to-do-about-it_us_57bcbc22e4b007f1819a1070#_ftnref8.

4. "Climate Change And Your Food: Ten Facts," *FAO*, accessed February 24, 2019, http://www.fao.org/news/story/en/item/356770/icode/.

5. "Key Facts On Food Loss And Waste You Should Know!" *Food And Agriculture Organization Of The United Nations*, accessed February 24, 2019, http://www.fao.org/save-food/resources/keyfindings/en/

6. Jose Graziano da Silva, "Reducing Food Loss and Waste Is Essential," *iWitness News*, March 1, 2019, https://www.iwnsvg.com/2018/07/26/reducing-food-loss-and-waste-is-essential/.

7. "Companies Can Help Reduce Food Loss And Waste Dramatically," *State Of Green*, August 28, 2018, https://stateofgreen.com/en/partners/state-of-green/news/new-bcg-report-companies-can-help-reduce-food-loss-and-waste-dramatically/.

8. Story Hinckley, "France Was The First Country To Ban Supermarkets From Throwing Away Unused Food — And The World Is Taking Notice," *Business Insider*, January 6, 2018, https://www.businessinsider.com/how-france-became-a-global-leader-in-curbing-food-waste-2018-1.

9. Princeton University, "A more potent greenhouse gas than carbon dioxide, methane emissions will leap as Earth warms," (Princeton University, March 27, 2014), www.sciencedaily.com/releases/2014/03/140327111724.htm.

10. FAO, "Key Facts On Food Loss And Waste You Should Know!"; Princeton University, "A more potent greenhouse gas than carbon dioxide."

11. Hinckley, "France Was The First Country To Ban Supermarkets From Throwing Away Unused Food — And The World Is Taking Notice."

12. Esben Hegnsholt et al., "Tackling The 1.6-Billion-Ton Food Loss And Waste Crisis," *BCG*, August 20, 2018, https://www.bcg.com/publications/2018/tackling-1.6-billion-ton-food-loss-and-waste-crisis.aspx.

13. Emma Cosgrove, "4 Technologies Tackling Food Waste In The Supply Chain," *Supply Chain Dive*, September 12, 2018, https://www.supplychaindive.com/news/4-technologies-food-waste-in-supply-chain/532155/.

14. Cosgrove, "4 Technologies Tackling Food Waste In The Supply Chain."

15. Cosgrove, "4 Technologies Tackling Food Waste In The Supply Chain."

16. Tom Huddleston Jr., "This Bill Gates-Backed Start-Up Is Fighting World Hunger By Making Your Avocados Last Longer," *CNBC*, December 31, 2018, https://www.cnbc.com/2018/12/31/bill-gates-backed-apeel-sciences-makes-fruit-avocados-last-longer.html.

17. Caitlin Dewey, "This Start-Up Can Make Avocados Last Twice As Long Before Going Bad," *Washington Post*, June 19, 2018, https://www.washingtonpost.com/news/wonk/wp/2018/06/19/this-start-up-can-make-avocados-last-twice-as-long-before-going-bad/?noredirect=on&utm_term=.cd107ef51cfe.

18. Huddleston Jr., "This Bill Gates-Backed Start-Up Is Fighting World Hunger By Making Your Avocados Last Longer."

19. "Our Story," *FRESHPAPER*, accessed February 24, 2019, https://www.freshglow.co/freshpaperstory.

20. Chris Koger, "Mission Produce Rolls Out Hazel Tech Avocado Program," *The Packer*, January 14, 2019, https://www.thepacker.com/article/mission-produce-rolls-out-hazel-tech-avocado-program.

21. "About," *Farther Farms*, accessed February 24, 2019, https://www.fartherfarms.com/about-us.

22. Leanna Garfield, "Spray This Invisible, Edible Coating On Produce And It Could Last Five Times Longer," *Business Insider*, October 16, 2017, https://www.businessinsider.com/coating-extends-produce-life-apeel-sciences-2017-10.

23. FAO, "Key Facts On Food Loss And Waste You Should Know!"

24. Emma Cosgrove, "Hellofresh Taps Spoiler Alert To Cut Food Waste By 65%," *Agfundernews*, April 17, 2018, https://agfundernews.com/hellofresh-food-waste-spoiler-alert.html.

25. "Yieldwise Food Loss," *The Rockefeller Foundation*, accessed February 24, 2019, https://www.rockefellerfoundation.org/our-work/initiatives/yieldwise/.

26. The Rockefeller Foundation, "Yieldwise Food Loss."

27. The Rockefeller Foundation, "Yieldwise Food Loss."

28. Dewey, "This Start-Up Can Make Avocados Last Twice As Long Before Going Bad."

29. The Rockefeller Foundation, "Yieldwise Food Loss."

30. R. J. HODGES, J. C. BUZBY and B. BENNETT, "Postharvest Losses And Waste In Developed And Less Developed Countries: Opportunities To Improve Resource Use", *The Journal Of Agricultural Science* 149, no. 1 (2010): 37-45, doi:10.1017/s0021859610000936.

31. Brian Macleod, "Biofortification: The Art Of Improving Food," *The Western Producer*, December 27, 2018, https://www.producer.com/2018/12/biofortification-the-art-of-improving-food/.

32. Cosgrove, "Hellofresh Taps Spoiler Alert To Cut Food Waste By 65%."

33. Cosgrove, "Hellofresh Taps Spoiler Alert To Cut Food Waste By 65%."

34. Jacqueline Parisi, "How Hellofresh Managed To Donate Over 1 Million Meals," *The Fresh Times*, April 17, 2018, https://blog.hellofresh.com/food-waste-statistics/.

35. BSR, *Analysis Of U.S. Food Waste Among Food Manufacturers, Retailers, And Restaurants*, Analysis Of U.S. Food Waste Among Food Manufacturers, Retailers, And Restaurants (Food Marketing Institute, Grocery Manufacturers Association, and National Restaurant Association, 2014), http://www.foodwastealliance.org/wp-content/uploads/2014/11/FWRA_BSR_Tier3_FINAL.pdf.

36. Cosgrove, "4 Technologies Tackling Food Waste In The Supply Chain."

37. Cosgrove, "4 Technologies Tackling Food Waste In The Supply Chain."

38. Cosgrove, "4 Technologies Tackling Food Waste In The Supply Chain."

39. "Real Time Food Quality Decisions," *Impact Vision*, accessed February 24, 2019, https://www.impactvi.com.

40. Cosgrove, "4 Technologies Tackling Food Waste In The Supply Chain."

41. Parvez Musani, "The Tech That'S Bringing Fresher Groceries To You," *Walmart Today*, March 1, 2018, https://blog.walmart.com/innovation/20180301/eden-the-tech-thats-bringing-fresher-groceries-to-you.

42. Musani, "The Tech That'S Bringing Fresher Groceries To You."

43. Hegnsholt et al., "Tackling The 1.6-Billion-Ton Food Loss And Waste Crisis."

44. Julie Smith, *PACSA Monthly Food Price Barometer: MARCH 2017*, PACSA (Petermaritzburg: PACSA, March 2017), http://www.pacsa.org.za/images/food_barometer/2017/March_2017_PACSA_monthly_food_price_barometer.pdf.

CHAPTER 10: THE DIGITIZATION OF THE FOOD SUPPLY (BLOCK)CHAIN

1. Jenny McTaggart, "Grocers Embrace Blockchain In New Era Of Transparency," *Progressive Grocer*, February 16, 2018, https://progressivegrocer.com/grocers-embrace-blockchain-new-era-transparency.

2. McTaggart, "Grocers Embrace Blockchain In New Era Of Transparency."

3. McTaggart, "Grocers Embrace Blockchain In New Era Of Transparency."

4. McTaggart, "Grocers Embrace Blockchain In New Era Of Transparency."

5. McTaggart, "Grocers Embrace Blockchain In New Era Of Transparency."

6. Sylvain Charlebois, "How Blockchain Technology Could Transform The Food Industry," *The Conversation*, December 19, 2017, https://theconversation.com/how-blockchain-technology-could-transform-the-food-industry-89348.

7. Alec Ross, *Industries of The Future* (New York: Simon & Schuster, 2017), 98-106.

8. Alec Ross, *Industries of The Future* (New York: Simon & Schuster, 2017), 98-106.

9. Bettina Warburg, "How The Blockchain Will Radically Transform The Economy," (Presentation, TEDSummit, June 2016).

10. Andy Hoffman and Ruben Munsterman, "Dreyfus Teams With Banks for First Agriculture Blockchain Trade," *Bloomberg*, January 22, 2018, https://www.bloomberg.com/news/articles/2018-01-22/dreyfus-teams-with-banks-for-first-agriculture-blockchain-trade.

11. Hoffman and Munsterman, "Dreyfus Teams With Banks."

12. "Financial Times," *Financial Times*, accessed February 24, 2019, https://www.ft.com/content/22b2ac1e-fd1a-11e7-a492-2c9be7f3120a.

13. Hoffman and Munsterman, "Dreyfus Teams With Banks."

14. Hoffman and Munsterman, "Dreyfus Teams With Banks."

15. Hoffman and Munsterman, "Dreyfus Teams With Banks."

16. Hoffman and Munsterman, "Dreyfus Teams With Banks."

17. McTaggart, "Grocers Embrace Blockchain In New Era Of Transparency."

18. Russell Redman, "More Retailers Join IBM Food Trust Network," *Supermarket News,* October 8, 2019, https://www.supermarketnews.com/food-safety/more-retailers-join-ibm-food-trust-network.

19. Redman, "More Retailers Join IBM Food Trust Network."

20. Redman, "More Retailers Join IBM Food Trust Network."

21. "About The Sustainable Development Goals," *United Nations Sustainable Development,* accessed February 24, 2019, https://www.un.org/sustainabledevelopment/sustainable-development-goals/.

CONCLUSION: THE FUTURE OF FOOD DISRUPTION

1. Vanessa Ramirez, "The 6 Ds Of Tech Disruption: A Guide To The Digital Economy," *Singularity Hub,* November 22, 2016, https://singularityhub.com/2016/11/22/the-6-ds-of-tech-disruption-a-guide-to-the-digital-economy/#sm.001ymf7kn100bffsyv92af5pig16v.

2. Ramirez, "The 6 Ds Of Tech Disruption: A Guide To The Digital Economy."

3. Ramirez, "The 6 Ds Of Tech Disruption: A Guide To The Digital Economy."

4. Ramirez, "The 6 Ds Of Tech Disruption: A Guide To The Digital Economy."

5. Ramirez, "The 6 Ds Of Tech Disruption: A Guide To The Digital Economy."

6. Ramirez, "The 6 Ds Of Tech Disruption: A Guide To The Digital Economy."

7. Ramirez, "The 6 Ds Of Tech Disruption: A Guide To The Digital Economy."

8. Dr. Prabhu Pingali, interview with author, December 6, 2018.

9. Aldo Leopold, "The Land Ethic"(1948), in *A Sand County Almanac and Sketches Here and There, 2nd ed.* (New York: Oxford University Press, 1968), 215, **quoted in** Dan Barber, *The Third Plate* (New York: The Penguin Press, 2014), 178.

10. Dan Barber, *The Third Plate* (New York: The Penguin Press, 2014), 178.

Printed in Poland
by Amazon Fulfillment
Poland Sp. z o.o., Wrocław

86694211R00170